D0174499

dealing with
the tough stuff

THE SOCIAL VENTURE NETWORK SERIES

RETIRÉ DE LA COLLECTION UNIVERSELLE

Bibliothèque et Archives nationales du Québec

dealing with the tough stuff

PRACTICAL WISDOM FOR RUNNING
A VALUES-DRIVEN BUSINESS

Margot Fraser

Lisa Lorimer

BK

Berrett–Koehler Publishers, Inc.
San Francisco
a BK Business book

Copyright © 2009 by Margot Fraser and Lisa Lorimer

All rights reserved. No part of this publication may be reproduced, distributed, or transmitted in any form or by any means, including photocopying, recording, or other electronic or mechanical methods, without the prior written permission of the publisher, except in the case of brief quotations embodied in critical reviews and certain other noncommercial uses permitted by copyright law. For permission requests, write to the publisher, addressed "Attention: Permissions Coordinator," at the address below.

Berrett-Koehler Publishers, Inc.
235 Montgomery Street, Suite 650
San Francisco, CA 94104-2916
Tel: (415) 288-0260   Fax: (415) 362-2512   www.bkconnection.com

Ordering Information

Quantity sales. Special discounts are available on quantity purchases by corporations, associations, and others. For details, contact the "Special Sales Department" at the Berrett-Koehler address above.

Individual sales. Berrett-Koehler publications are available through most bookstores. They can also be ordered directly from Berrett-Koehler: Tel: (800) 929-2929; Fax: (802) 864-7626; www.bkconnection.com.

Orders for college textbook/course adoption use. Please contact Berrett-Koehler: Tel: (800) 929-2929; Fax: (802) 864-7626.

Orders by U.S. trade bookstores and wholesalers. Please contact Ingram Publisher Services: Tel: (800) 509-4887; Fax: (800) 838-1149; E-mail: customer.service@ingrampublisherservices.com; or visit www.ingrampublisherservices.com/Ordering for details about electronic ordering.

Berrett-Koehler and the BK logo are registered trademarks of Berrett-Koehler Publishers, Inc.

Printed in the United States of America

Berrett-Koehler books are printed on long-lasting acid-free paper. When it is available, we choose paper that has been manufactured by environmentally responsible processes. These may include using trees grown in sustainable forests, incorporating recycled paper, minimizing chlorine in bleaching, or recycling the energy produced at the paper mill.

Library of Congress Cataloging-in-Publication Data
Fraser, Margot, 1929-
    Dealing with the tough stuff : practical wisdom for running a values-driven business / Margot Fraser, Lisa Lorimer. — 1st ed.
        p. cm. — (Social venture network series)
    Includes index.
    ISBN 978-1-57675-665-2 (pbk. : alk. paper)
    1. Business ethics. 2. Management—Moral and ethical aspects. I. Lorimer, Lisa. II. Title.
    HF5387.F7375 2009
    174'.4—dc22   2009029930

FIRST EDITION
14 13 12 11 10 09   10 9 8 7 6 5 4 3 2 1

*This book is dedicated to some incredible people,
my employees and customers, who taught me
what business is all about.*

Margot Fraser

*This book is dedicated to the amazing leaders
who are trying to do a very radical thing: use their
companies as a way to change their part of the world.
And we know, this is so much easier said than done.*

Lisa Lorimer

Contents

Letter from the Editor of the Social Venture Network Series

Talk to just about any member of Social Venture Network who runs a business, and you'll likely learn that pursuing the triple bottom line of people, planet, and profit isn't just personally more rewarding than following the single bottom line of profit—it's also often more profitable. Yet if you ask that same entrepreneur whether integrating social and environmental values into her core business principles and practices has made running her business easier, you'll hear a different story.

As Lisa Lorimer and Margot Fraser write in this remarkable little book, "Nothing is ever smooth in business. Things rarely run exactly as they should without challenges that keep you up at night." Truth to tell, the triple bottom line may add to the challenges.

Every business decision, whatever the circumstances, is a matter of trade-offs. Running a socially responsible business imposes a whole new set of trade-offs:

- Customers may demand better service than your overworked staff can provide. How can you satisfy both stakeholders' interests?
- A commitment to lighten the company's environmental footprint may require retraining staff and increasing costs in the short run. If you have limited cash on hand, will that commitment have to wait?
- Guaranteeing quality products may pose financial challenges when the price of a key ingredient dramatically rises. Is cutting your own take-home pay the only way to honor your commitment to quality?

Situations like these, and thousands of others, bedevil every socially responsible business leader. In the pages that follow, Margot and Lisa explore such questions in the broader context of the difficult challenges that face *any* small or midsized business—from the very personal perspective of the business owner.

Dealing with the Tough Stuff is an intensely personal book. This is a sort of "true confessions" from the world of business, so very unlike the case studies found in business school courses. This is raw reality, laid bare for you and me by two remarkable business leaders who bear the scars of their success. Beginning with the authors' own brutally honest stories, and encompassing a host of others from business founders and owners who share their own painful and embarrassing difficulties, this book will help you negotiate the minefield of financial, emotional, and personal challenges that will inevitably arise as you build your business.

If you're in business, or thinking of starting a company, "for the fun of it," please read this book. When you hit those unavoidable bumps in the road and it's not fun anymore, you'll think back to one of the many memorable stories in this book, or some insightful comment by the authors, and you'll get through the crisis with a little bit less anxiety.

If *Dealing with the Tough Stuff* had been available to me many years ago when my business was on the ropes, I'm sure I would have gotten a lot more sleep.

MAL WARWICK
Berkeley, California
October 2009

Preface

Hundreds, perhaps thousands, of good business books are on the market today, so why do you need this one? You need it because very few people talk about how tough it is to run a business. Very few business books offer suggestions on how to jump the hurdles that arise as you grow your business. This book answers questions about how an entrepreneur can stay balanced, sane, and profitable while running a values-driven company that focuses on people, planet, and profit. This is not a book that tells you how to *avoid* the tough stuff; it is a book about how to *deal* with the tough stuff when it inevitably comes along.

In order to write the book, we both told our stories about the challenges of running businesses. Then we searched for a small group of entrepreneurs, working in various sectors, who would be willing to talk about the difficult times they've had in running their businesses. We looked for business leaders who could see clearly, speak truthfully, and laugh loudly. These leaders had to be brave and honest enough to go beyond the PR and tell us what it was really like. In the end, we chose five contributors: Carol Berry, cofounder and CEO of Putney Pasta, an all-natural gourmet pasta company; Gary Hirshberg, president, chairman, and CEO of Stonyfield Farm, the world's leading organic yogurt producer; Joe O'Connell, founding owner of Creative Machines, a nine-person company that makes interactive museum exhibits, public art, and simple machines to help the neediest people worldwide; Marie Wilson, president of the Ms. Foundation for Women and founder of the White

House Project, a progressive nonpartisan organization whose mission is to put more women in positions of leadership; and Tom Raffio, president and CEO of Northeast Delta Dental, a provider of dental benefits to individuals and organizations in New Hampshire, Vermont, and Maine.

These contributors offered differing perspectives in terms of gender, age, industry, and geographic region. The contributors are weighted a little heavier in "product" companies, but they also represent the service sector, nonprofits, and the arts. Some of our contributors are still running their businesses, one almost lost her business, another is trying to find a steady cash-flow product to stabilize his company, and some found unique ways to sell their businesses when it was time to move on. Despite the differences among the contributors and their businesses, the core structures that helped these folks through the tough times were surprisingly similar: create an advisory board, own your numbers, and take care of the leader. We created two extended practical wisdom sections on creating an advisory board and owning your numbers. The practical tips are geared toward taking care of you, the leader.

Whether you are a new or seasoned entrepreneur, you will need help dealing with the difficult situations that come along in business while also staying close to your values-driven mission. This book offers practical wisdom and useful tips on how to stay sane in an increasingly difficult business world. The best way to use this book is to think of us sitting with you at your kitchen table, telling stories and offering advice over a cup of coffee. We are not the experts; we are fellow travelers who have figured out how to make the tough stuff a little easier. In this book, the president of a manufacturing company survives an accident at her plant; the CEO of a service company talks about the Goliath of consolidation; the head of a company faces an employee lawsuit after a consultant makes a bad move; a nonprofit leader asks for money for her organization's mission while not being sure she can pay that month's rent; a small business owner, brilliant at product development, learns about the importance of bookkeeping; and the head of a successful company wakes up at three in the morning, worrying about payroll. Each one of us writes about being on the verge of burnout, feeling scared, overwhelmed, and lonely. Telling the truth in these stories has made us better leaders, and we believe it can do the same for you. Some of what we say will resonate with you—it will open a door, spark an idea. Keep those parts of the book and use them. Other suggestions will feel like trying on an itchy sweater that doesn't fit. Leave those suggestions until another time or share them with another businessperson who needs help.

These are times of great change and uncertainty in our economy, and many people are looking for meaning in their lives. We are looking for ways to connect to our communities, provide livable jobs for ourselves and our stakeholders, and, most importantly, find meaning in our work. With a firm resolve to adhere to the "three Ps" (people, planet, profit), you, as a socially responsible business leader, are in a unique position. You are acting in a radical way by using business as a tool to create the change you want to see in the world. Our intention is to help you do this. Whether you are contemplating striking out on your own, are already running a business, or are working in an organization that is interested in more than the next quarterly profit report, this book is for you.

Acknowledgments

We would like to express our sincere appreciation and gratitude to the many people who worked with us in bringing forth the stories and ideas for *Dealing with the Tough Stuff*.

First and foremost to Suzanne Kingsbury, without whom this book would still be a very interesting collection of papers piled high on the dining room table. Her terrific sense of humor, constant support, clarity of thinking, and amazing ability to discern a clear and compelling narrative from our tangled stories has been the driving force of this book.

To Johanna Vondeling from Berrett-Koehler Publishers, who encouraged us to write this book because she wanted to read it, and to Deb Nelson from Social Venture Network, who started us on this path of becoming authors in the SVN book series.

To Lori Hanau who did a wonderful job in the interview process with many of our contributors, and to Nancy Doyle who transcribed all those hours of tapes.

To Leslie Kelly, Steve Mintz, Pat Beu, Carol Berry, David Berge, Rick Slater, Ricky Berger, Jan Eastman, Dawn Mcgee, and Elizabeth Crook, who were there throughout the various tough stuff for Lisa.

To Glenn Sleezer, first accountant; Mary Jones, first employee; June Embury, first partner; Melanie Grimes, early customer; and Walter Georis, the young man on the escalator, who have been there throughout Margot's stories.

And most especially to Stephen Schoen and Meg Donahue, who have supported us, pushed us, laughed with us, questioned us, and helped us through this past year of writing.

To all, we say a heartfelt thank you!

Telling the truth about values-based business

The tough stuff is normal. If you are running a company and feel stressed and overwhelmed, you are not alone. Staying committed to your mission, making a profit, growing your business to fit the marketplace, dealing with trends that are out of your control, learning how to deal with the "big guys," and playing the role of CEO are all difficult balls to juggle. There is no magic wand to make it all better. But when other entrepreneurs tell their stories about how they managed, when they share tips and practical wisdom, it can help enormously. The impetus for this book came when we (Lisa and Margot) were both invited to speak to a group of new entrepreneurs at a green business event. We told the stories of how our businesses grew, including the times we made mistakes and what we learned from them. We exposed ourselves as entrepreneurs who had sometimes tried and failed. Warts and all, we shared the experiences we thought would be most useful to someone starting on the path of socially responsible business. The entrepreneurs listening loved what we had to say, and they encouraged us to share these stories with a wider audience. They gave us the courage to write this book.

We wrote this book so you would know that when you face the tough stuff and feel isolated in your business, you are not alone. Many people have been in that boat with you. As business owners, we tend to put on our game faces and pretend everything is fine. Really, we wake up at 3:00 a.m. worrying, eat horribly, drink too much coffee, pour ourselves an extra glass of wine, and don't have time to exercise or meditate. We try to leave our business issues at the door when we go home only to find those issues creeping under the doorsill. Our partners, families, and friends can love us, take us to dinner, and rub our tense shoulders, but unless they've had the experience of running a business, they can't really know how to help. So, ultimately, we stop paying enough attention to our partners and kids. We run values-driven companies, yet we stop looking at our own values. We try to create a better world, yet we are not taking care of our personal worlds. But most of us have no place where we can tell the truth. In order to grow, we have to tell untruths, to position ourselves, especially in the early years, to look bigger than we are in order to attract customers, employees, and suppliers. We add "& Company" to our names even when the only other breathing animal in the office is a Persian cat asleep in the corner. When working with a fellow sole operator, we refer to our work together as "two organizations collaborating" to give the impression that we bring more resources to the work than we actually do. As we grow, we tend to continue this pattern of untruths. As our companies grow, our need to put on our best faces and pretend to the world that we are "doing great!" grows, too.

There are valid business reasons for putting on that game face and not telling the whole truth. As socially responsible business leaders who are committed to a triple bottom line of people, planet, and profit we are expected to see beyond the problems of today and create the dreams of the future. It would never be appropriate to blurt out every truth, and in this book we are certainly not going to advocate adding truth serum to our morning coffee. We must publicly speak about our company's strengths, presenting a formidable presence to our competitors and positioning ourselves to attract customers, capital, and employees. But it is difficult for values-driven business leaders to have to create a web of untruths, half truths, and spin in order develop their companies. Hiding the truth can create an ecosystem that ultimately works against us, making it more difficult to reach out to each other and get the support we need to lead our companies and communities in healthy ways.

We do not intend to hide the truth when we start our businesses; we start our businesses with good intentions. We find a niche for our product or service, offer it at a fair price for the value proposition, and find customers as we begin to grow. We don't know that running a values-based business and trying to make a profit can sometimes feel mutually exclusive. What we are doing is pretty radical. We are trying to change the way business is done. We are striving to focus on the triple bottom line—people, planet and profit. We want to align our passion and values with work in our communities so that we can achieve positive change in the world. The only sane way we can do that is to find places where we can tell the truth. In order to truly be in our power and inspire a vibrant ecosystem that feeds our leaders rather than eats them, we need to find ways to be even more self-reflective and compassionate. We do this by sharing with others the challenges and stressors of running businesses. This book helps us ring a clear bell so that we connect rather than isolate. The two of us start by sharing our own stories, telling our own truth about where we started, what challenges arose, and how we survived.

The Fairy Tale of the Business-Owner Queen

■ LISA

I wanted to write this book because I was looking for ways that we, as businesspeople, can connect and share the truth about what it is like to run our companies. How can we get support to help us be stronger, better leaders in our values-based businesses? One of the things that appears to stop us is that we think other people know more than we do or that they don't have the same types of problems we have. We develop fairy tales about other business leaders and tell ourselves that everything came easily to them, and we are the only ones who have challenges and sometimes feel like failures. I wanted to speak lightheartedly about this problem, so I wrote my own fairy tale. I'll show you what my fairy tale looks like, and then I will tell my truth. Seeing the difference between fantasy and reality might help you feel less alone as an entrepreneur.

Once upon a time, a long, long time ago (in 1960) in a land far, far away (called Vermont), a girl-child was born as a fully formed Business-Owner Queen. She knew from birth everything there was to know about business. Her very first word was "debit," and her second word was "credit." She started her first business when she was four, sold that, and started her next one when she was twelve. When she was twenty-one, she had a Big Idea and started the company that was going to be the Big Idea she would do her whole adult life.

After sleeping soundly through the night, she always woke refreshed and renewed, and the fire and passion for the business *always* burned within her heart. Everybody loved her. Her customers never asked for deals, always paid their bills within terms, and always bought more every week. Her suppliers always extended extra terms. They never raised their prices and never short-shipped her on supplies. Her distributors never asked for additional margin or took an unauthorized chargeback. They always paid their bills early. Her employees always appreciated her. They came to work every day they were scheduled and never complained. Her board loved her, her lawyers loved her, her accountants loved her, her business partner loved her, and her bankers loved her. They never asked for her home as collateral. They always increased her line of credit whenever she asked. They never made her sweat her covenants and ratios.

This Business-Owner Queen never had to worry about money. She never ran out of cash, always had a positive cash flow, and took a full paycheck every week with increases every year. She always met payroll without concern, was profitable every year, and could take a price increase whenever she needed to.

Our Queen was written up in magazines and newspapers, was interviewed on television and radio, and was a congressional appointee to the White House Conference on Small Business. She met the president, fielded calls from her legislators, and was asked for her advice about laws that would help her succeed. She always stayed upbeat and positive with an open door.

Then one day she decided it was time to do something else, and the very next day she sold her company for lots and lots of money with no holdbacks or ongoing commitments. Now her phone rings all the time. She has been asked to run for the Senate. She serves on many paid boards, she has been called to write a book about her experiences, and . . .

All right, let's stop. Whew.

We can laugh about this, but enough of my true life story is in this fairy tale to make me *seem* like the Business-Owner Queen. In fact, my story is much more complex and the road much more difficult than this tale suggests. Knowing this, I still put other successful business owners into fairy tales, even though their roads were probably just as rocky as mine. We all do this to each other. What I really need to do is tell you my truth and share with you what really happened so we can learn together.

In order to run a business, particularly a values-based, socially responsible business, I had to deal with the tough stuff like everyone else. I learned to deal with this tough stuff early on. I grew up poor in a small town in southern Vermont. My single mom did the best she could raising three kids on a country teacher's salary. Because I was the oldest, it was my job, from a very early age, to cook dinner, lead the laundry brigade, and take care of the younger kids. For a number of years we lived in a tiny one-bedroom apartment. The bedroom was slightly larger than the double bed my sister and I shared. My mother slept on the couch in the living room, and my brother slept in the kitchen. Some nights it was so cold that we would all put on snowmobile suits and crawl into the same bed to keep warm. Sitting down at dinner with us one night, my uncle said, "Even JC couldn't do much with this amount of food." I remember wondering who JC was and not knowing until much later my uncle was referring to Jesus Christ, a man who could feed thousands of people with some fish and a little bit of bread.

Because we were so poor, the community in our small town stepped in to help, and perhaps my commitment to community building and creating local jobs began from this experience. The church held clothing drives and soon afterward, big, green bags of hand-me-downs would arrive on our front porch. My adult self is so appreciative of what people shared with us, but as a ten-year-old I was embarrassed. I wanted to go to work as soon as I could so I could have money to buy new pants. I had two pairs at a time, but they were never new.

When I was thirteen, I got a real job at the stables cleaning stalls and leading trail rides. I remember taking seven city people out on a ride on a nearby dirt road. It never occurred to me to have a plan in case something were to go wrong. And it did. As we rounded a corner, a herd of cattle, led by a charging bull, ran toward us. The horses bolted and left tourists everywhere—lying on the ground, tangled in trees, hanging sideways in saddles that had slipped off the horses' backs. I somehow stayed calm, settled each horse down, helped each rider remount, and led them all back to the barn. When I think back to this story, it's a metaphor for how I learned to stay calm during crises later.

School was a lifesaver for me. I attended a three-room schoolhouse with two grades per room. I would finish my first-grade work quickly and then go across the room and do the second-grade assignments. By sixteen I had finished high school. After dropping out of college (too much, too soon) I came back to Vermont and worked as a prep chef at a French restaurant owned by a female entrepreneur. Because she was such a powerful role model, it never occurred to me that I couldn't run a company.

At twenty-one I began what would be my long journey with Vermont Bread Company. I answered an ad in the local paper for a job at a tiny bakery in rural Vermont. The job had four requirements: be able to drive a truck, be good with people, be able to use a ten-key adding machine, and know the difference between a debit and a credit. I was from Vermont, I knew how to drive anything, I was mostly good with people, and I figured I would learn the rest. I found all sorts of crazy reasons to take home that silly adding machine until I got it, but to this day I don't know the difference between a debit and a credit. That is not to say I don't own my numbers. I know about margins, I know about costing, I can read a financial statement and tell you what is happening in the company and where the issues are, but I cannot do those accounting T-charts that tell you how to make ledger entries. Sometimes the entries are positive and sometimes they are negative, but I don't get it. I found out that you don't really need to know that to own your numbers, so I am lucky.

A few months after I started working at the bakery, we decided to make natural and organic bread. It sounds like an obvious idea today, but in the mid-1970s there were no organic breads in stores (and no organic certifications either). We thought it would be a Big Idea and all the store owners and suppliers would want to help us. Thinking we had a big idea was probably our first mistake. Instead they said, "No, you can't do it. The dough is too stiff for the mixing machines, the bread is too dense to be sliced, and if you put the product into a supermarket it will mold too quickly, so no."

But we went forward with our idea to make organic, natural bread anyway. We had the oven and the mixer, and we made bread just like you would from your grandmother's *Joy of Cooking* recipe. We started selling directly to consumers through the local farmers' market. We didn't know it, but we were making another mistake: an inconsistent product line. Every batch was different. We tested the bread to make sure it was tasty, and then we sold it. It wasn't until the 1980s that we remedied that and began to make every batch the same. We also made a mistake (twice) just in naming our company. At first the bakery was called Innisfree, named after the Yeats poem. Lovely name, but our customers would say, "What? Industry? Oh, yeah, the Vermont bread company." After a few years we renamed it Vermont Bread Company. But that was another mistake. When we became a national company, the Vermont name confused people. They tried to figure out how bread in Texas could be fresh if it came from Vermont. For that reason, we use our Rudi's Organic Bakery brand as our national brand.

The truth of growing my business from a tiny little bakery on a dirt road to the largest majority woman-owned business in Vermont is not that fairy tale. My house was on the line every day until the moment I sold the company. My relationship with my original bank was strained irreparably after I took over majority ownership. The bank added a large number of new covenants that were not in place when the previous man owned the company. We ran out of cash a lot, especially while we were growing. The last time I ran out of cash was the week before I sold the majority of my company.

As you can see, the real tale is more about believing in a good product, staying calm in the face of adversity, persevering through the tough stuff, and getting the help you need. It is nowhere near a fairy tale with magic wands and a queen's crown.

Surviving the Joys and Sorrows of the Birkenstock Adventure

■ **MARGOT**

I like to say, "I didn't found Birkenstock USA; it found me." It didn't start with a business plan to create a values-driven company; it started with my lifelong aching feet. While on a trip to Germany in 1966, I found a pair of sandals that weren't pretty to look at but were shaped like a foot. After three months of wearing them, my toes straightened out. All the exercises the foot doctor told me to do, like standing on a phone book and grabbing it with my toes (which made me feel like a hero if I did it for three minutes), I did automatically with these sandals. This was the spark for my company. It was the 1960s and all women's shoes were narrow and had pointed toes. Even the so-called healthy shoes still had heels. Because millions of women in the United States had painful feet, I thought it would be easy to get them into this marvelous footwear.

My then-husband and I wrote to the company in Germany that made the shoes, saying we'd like to sell them in the United States. After a long while someone from the company wrote back and agreed to our plan. The first shoes were sent to our house via parcel post. My husband had owned an import business, importing modern furniture and implements for the home. He had started in a retail store, moved into wholesale, and finally sold the business. Based on his experience, he told me to start wholesale right away. Since one shoe store in our hometown sold somewhat comfortable footwear, it was my first sales call. I walked in through the back door as the owner was coming out of the stockroom with boxes of shoes under his arm, heading toward a customer. I showed him what I had, and he didn't even stop—he just marched by, saying he could never sell anything like that in his store. That was the end of my first sales call. My husband thought it would be good to have an appointment next time, so he called someone he knew at a European-style shoe store and set up a meeting. The man was very polite, so this time it took over an hour and a half for us to get the same message as before: he could never sell anything like our shoes in his store. After getting turned down by shoe stores, we approached podiatrists, who thought we would put them out of business. I knew I could learn a lot of things, but I didn't think I could ever learn to sell.

Our turning point came when a friend, who was connected with the emerging health-food field, mentioned that the Health Food Association was having a national convention close by in San Francisco and might still have space. Two weeks later I was behind a table with a red tablecloth, displaying our shoes. I showed the sandals to everyone, told my story, and asked people to try them on. These health-food store owners understood the value of the shoes because they were on their feet all day, standing behind the cash registers in their shops. One health-food store owner hobbled through the aisles of the show in her nylons, carrying her uncomfortable shoes. We were not supposed to directly solicit, but I couldn't resist. The woman tried on a pair and bought them despite her husband's protests about how ugly they were and how many other pairs of shoes were in her closet at home.

On the last day of the show, the same woman returned to my booth and took three more pairs of sandals to sell in her store. She made sure all three were in her size so if they didn't sell, she could just wear them herself. Later, she would become my business partner. That's how we got started in 1967, selling shoes to health-food stores. By 1970 my marriage had fallen apart, and I left the business and moved to San Francisco. I supported myself in the profession for which I was trained: dressmaking and dress design. But shoe customers started calling me to say, "Hey, your ex is not keeping up the business. As a matter of fact, he left the country. He left behind a manager without authority to carry on, and now the shoes are beginning to sell and no new shoes are coming in." I didn't have any money because my divorce wasn't settled yet, so I went into partnership with the health-food store owner and her husband. They worked in San Rafael, and I set up our company just above their shop. This worked like a business incubator. I paid $25 a month in rent, and we shared a part-time secretary and stockboy. We didn't sell to our first shoe store until 1973 when a customer complained to her local shoe store that she shouldn't have to go to a food store to buy shoes. By the time I sold the company in 2002, we had two hundred employees and over $120 million in sales.

Who would have known that I would wind up being the head of a successful company like Birkenstock? I grew up in

Berlin during the war. The principal of my elementary school was an old Prussian lady—anti-Nazi, like my parents—and she instilled in me the belief that girls were capable of anything and should follow their dreams. My mother thought that was all ridiculous feminist stuff, but my father thought it was safer for me to stay at that school than switch to the Nazi-controlled high school, so I got to stay. During my last year of school, the city was already very damaged by bombs, but the school still offered counseling for children about their careers. Though I hadn't told anyone, I already knew I wanted to go into business, so I was enrolled in a secretarial school. My father and I went to the counselor with all my grades and examples of my embroideries, crafts, and artwork. The counselor said to my father, "It would be a pity for your daughter to go to a secretarial school. She has artistic talents. She should do something with her hands where she can see a finished product afterward." She suggested a prestigious dressmaking school in Berlin.

When we were out on the street, I said to my father, "I'm not going to do that. I want to be an international merchant." I had read an idealistic book about German merchants overseas. It profiled merchants who imported coffee, cotton, tobacco, and other commodities. It also explained how international trade promoted peace and understanding of foreign cultures. I told my father that's what I wanted to do: I wanted people to learn that not all Germans were bad. My father said to me, "My dear, you could never do that as a woman. Didn't you notice that book was all about men? All you can hope for is to type letters for somebody else." It was true at the time. Of course, that's not what I had in mind, but I followed the counselor's advice and wound up in dressmaking school. It turned out to be a great choice—a tremendous help for my life!

The dressmaking school was excellent. From day one the instructors taught us to come up with our own ideas; they never had us copy anything. We created our own embroidery designs, even our own dress patterns. During this time, the war was getting worse. I could not finish school because the building became a hospital for wounded soldiers. I had learned enough to be able to sew well, and I knew how to make dress patterns, which was a very valuable skill. Money could not buy anything at that time. We had become a barter society, and my skills were good "currency." When we were able to get out of the city and move to a village in the country, I made clothes for the farmers' families, and they paid me with eggs and butter. What I did not know then was that this made me an entrepreneur. I was not yet sixteen.

Once the war was over, I went to a school for applied art in Bremen. I was seventeen, the youngest student ever enrolled. But that was another two-year program from which I did not graduate. In 1948 we had a currency reform in Germany, and our money then became worth only ten cents to the dollar. Our savings were gone and my father was unemployed, so we could not afford my tuition. However, two of my friends and I decided that by then we knew more than the teachers, and we set up a dressmaking salon together.

We ran our own business for two years until a customer encouraged me to go into business for myself. Bremen was under U.S. occupation, and a resident had to be only twenty-one years old to apply for any business license. I waited until my birthday and registered the very next day. My business did well, but I could not see a future for myself in Germany. I wanted to go overseas. I had no connections in the United States, but Canada was still taking immigrants. I went to the Canadian Consulate to find out what I needed to do and was told that if I could find a job in Canada, I could get a visa. I was in the waiting room for a long time, and I read through all the newspapers. There were some German-language newspapers, and I found out that the president of the German Club in Toronto was a ladies' tailor. I copied his name and address, and I wrote to him about whether he could help me put an ad in the newspaper so I could look for a job. Lo and behold, he wrote back and said although he couldn't promise a long-term job, he needed somebody for four or five months, and if that was enough for me to take a risk, then I could have a visa. That letter came in November. (I know it was November because on my mother's birthday I went back to the consulate. All my aunts thought I was a bad girl for not attending my mother's birthday party.) By December 31, 1951, at the age of twenty-two, I was traveling overseas on a boat all by myself.

I arrived in Canada in the middle of January 1952. There I was in the New World, free from all the restrictions that had hampered me and open to all that was to come. I hardly spoke the language, all I had was $25 in my pocket and a promise of a few months' pay, but I was excited! What a chance for a new beginning. I can still feel the sense of exhilaration that came over me when our train finally pulled into the station in Toronto. Fresh snow had fallen overnight, and the sun came out bright and clear in the morning. I took it as a good omen.

At the time, I had no idea that the dream of that little girl in bomb-struck Berlin to become an international merchant would come true one day! I expected new difficulties to come my way, but I felt that I would be able to handle them when they did. Luck had smiled on me so far, and I hoped it would continue. I promised myself right then and there to tread lightly on this earth, to let life unfold and never to get too stuck on particular results. My experiences in the war taught me that you can never really own anything—everything in life is only on loan. With that lesson, I survived the joys and sorrows of my Birkenstock adventure.

What We Learned

We both wish we could go back and talk to our younger selves. In a sense, that is what we are doing in writing this book: sending a message in a bottle back to ourselves when we were there. Here we provide conversations with leaders who speak plainly about facing the tough stuff. As Margot keeps reminding us, this is not an answer book or a how-to book, it is a book about staying resilient and flexible even when we feel like everything is crashing down around us. It is about trying to see clearly and truthfully in the midst of real complexity. It is about understanding how the outer ecosystems of our companies and the inner ecosystems of ourselves are interrelated. We hope this book helps others who are in the same shoes we walked in years ago.

1

Conquering cash

Did you look at the chapter titles or flip through the book, skimming the headlines until you found the word "cash"? Welcome! You are the reader we are writing to, and this is the topic we assumed would get your attention first. If you ask entrepreneurs to name the toughest, most stressful aspect of running their companies, cash is almost always at the top of the list. It's the King of stressors.

In this chapter, we talk frankly about how we stayed focused on cash while balancing our values with the realities of meeting payroll. Lisa and Margot talk about the importance of knowing when to be frugal and creative ways to deal with inventory and payment terms. Gary Hirshberg of Stonyfield Farm explains that all problems are really cash problems and how that can be a unique challenge for values-based businesses. Joe O'Connell of Creative Machines explains the importance of a steady moneymaker in a business that makes custom products. And Marie Wilson, a social entrepreneur at the Ms. Foundation and the White House Project, shows how to look beyond the money to the vision and how you can find a way for the two to meet. We also give you a step-by-step guide to owning your numbers (and sometimes ducking them when you are stressed) and finding ways to get the help you need.

In a business that's values based, finding the balance between people, planet, and profit (cash!) is more complicated when there isn't enough cash. Hopefully this chapter will provide you with useful information to deal with this sometimes painful reality.

Cash Is King

■ **LISA**

About five years before I sold the majority of my company, I attended an executive education program at Harvard Business School. On the final day, my accounting professor told us that after all the time we spent in class and all the tuition we paid, we really needed to know only one thing. He said it was the most important piece of information we could take with us. He held up a large sign written in black marker that said "Cash Is King." We laughed and agreed. A simple sign that made us laugh, yet the idea is not so simple to deal with when we are in the midst of running a business.

I believe that perhaps the most valuable business practice is owning your numbers. Nowadays, I give talks to business groups and do one-on-one consulting about how important it is to understand your numbers. I tell business owners they can use their numbers to inform their decisions about what is most important and what to do next. I say that with a little practice, a calculator, and someone they can sit down with who will ask questions and help them find answers, all entrepreneurs can learn their numbers. These things are all true, and they help a lot. But there were times when I knew what the numbers meant, how to interpret them, and how to impact them, and yet despite that knowledge, I didn't have the courage to look at them. I could not stand seeing the negative balance growing in the checkbook, and I would leave my newly printed financial statements from the previous month unopened in my in-box for days. Every time I walked past the statements, my heart would beat faster and my stomach would hurt. I tried to tell myself that in order to stay in my bubble—in order to call customers, stay upbeat, and remain positive for the rest of the staff—I needed to ignore my financial problems. But that was never a long-term solution. In order to move my company forward, I always had to turn around and face those numbers.

In dealing with cash, I sometimes found it difficult to match my values with my actions. When cash was tight (or nonexistent), it made sense for me not to take a paycheck and to put my personal expenses on credit cards, whose balances kept increasing. We all know that is what you do when you run a company. But when I tell that side of the story, it is the Hero's Journey—I made a personal sacrifice to make it all work, and isn't that grand? The truth is, when there wasn't enough cash, my story wasn't pretty. When cash was particularly tight, I printed checks on a Friday, held them until the following week or the week after that, ducked phone calls from my suppliers while continuing to place orders, and then sent out checks only to the ones who yelled the loudest and threatened to cut us off. The stress of running out of cash was compounded because our core company values—Respect, Tell the Truth, and Keep Your Word—were all violated as I juggled everything to keep the company running.

Running a values-driven business is about trying to keep track of the multiple bottom lines and knowing that one part of the equation sometimes has to take precedence. It doesn't mean that we are perfect or even perfectly aligned with all our values all the time.

Forecasting Sales and Cash Flow Without a Crystal Ball

■ MARGOT

Very early on I had an experience that showed me the importance of doing my numbers myself and truly understanding how money came in and flowed out. When I started Birkenstock USA, Mr. Birkenstock in Germany gave me a $6,000 credit to purchase product. Unfortunately, that was not enough to get the company off the ground—we needed operating capital. My partners at the health-food store signed for a $6,000 loan at our local bank, but pretty soon, that amount wasn't enough either. That's when our accountant initiated me into the mysterious world of obtaining credit. I am forever grateful to him. He showed me how a cash-flow statement was done. It was an eye-opener. I realized that if I could do this, it would help me understand the business, so I took the statement home and worked on it. I was afraid the accountant was too optimistic and the loan officer wouldn't believe the figures, so I played with the numbers, shaving off money here and there and being more conservative with our projected sales growth. Then I was able to convince our loan officer to extend us the credit we needed. It helped enormously that I did this myself, by hand, with a calculator and a pen, not with a computer that worked it all out for me.

I was so excited by working with my own numbers that I searched for a seminar on the subject. I found a three-day event in San Jose, quite a distance from us. I took our key employee with me because I thought it was so important. We were only three at the time, but for our size it was a considerable expense. It proved to be worth it. My people could now understand why it was important to save money wherever we could, and I didn't have to fight them with my "stingy" notions.

Our accountant and the loan officer were helpful with cash flow when we began the business, but my ignorance saved me as much as anything else. I didn't understand how the footwear industry operated when we started, and that was fortunate because we did something unprecedented in the industry that enabled us to get cash, as underfunded as we were. We gave retailers a 5 percent discount if they paid their bill within ten days. Several industry folks said I was making a mistake and "giving things away," but I just laughed. We had calculated our selling price so it would cover this discount, and the folks that paid net thirty days actually paid a premium. This helped a lot with cash flow.

On the flip side of the cash-flow coin was inventory. Inventory was where most of our cash went and where our cash came from when we made sales. To build our business, we stocked inventory in our warehouse at all times. No other shoe vendor was doing that. It meant retailers could order as few or as many pairs as they needed when they needed them. Nobody would have ordered a supply from us unknowns for delivery six months out, as was customary in the industry. Instead, we shifted the burden of carrying inventory onto our own shoulders. We had only three styles in very few color combinations, and the sandals didn't go out of style the next season, so this made the whole arrangement feasible.

Balancing inventory and cash is an ongoing battle that you have to keep your eyes on the whole time. Even when the inventory shows up on your balance sheet and gives you a profit on the books, if it eats up all your cash, and you can't make payroll on Friday, there is still a chance you could go out of business.

Over the years, our inventory grew to be very large as we added more styles and more colors. Trying to carry stock in the warehouse wound up being troublesome and stress producing.

As long as inventory sat in the warehouse, it just ate cash because we had to maintain it and pay continued interest on the money the bank loaned us to buy it. We could borrow only up to 50 percent of the inventory's value. We also had to forecast what our customers might need and factor in the two to three months it would take before we received the merchandise. I took home lots of reports and pored over them at night. Pretty soon we had several people working on these forecasts, and we had spent thousands of dollars on computer programs that were supposed to cure the problem. A crystal ball might have been more helpful.

Eventually, we had to scale down our in-stock offerings and put some of the inventory burden back on the shoulders of the retailers. They had to preorder seasonal sandals six months in advance as was the industry norm. Our mantra—"The right goods at the right time for our customers"—wound up eluding us forever. Though we were very dedicated to customer service, I knew if we endangered the health of our business in the process, our dedication wouldn't help our customers very much. Keeping our eyes on the numbers and making sure the numbers balanced helped everybody to prosper in the end.

No Matter What It's About, It's About Cash

■ **GARY, STONYFIELD FARM**

My story is one of constantly being out of cash or almost being out, so I learned the hard way that you have to keep your eye on your cash situation or you might be sacrificing your values, your business, and yourself to someone who has the ability to write a check. When entrepreneurs look for cash, they usually have to bring in investors, and I've watched a long list of entrepreneurs get derailed, fired, or brought to their knees by investors who come into their businesses and represent themselves as visionaries. This misrepresentation isn't always blatant or malicious, but investors who have made their money on good bets or on the backs of others and haven't actually built a business tend to bring unrealistic and unfair expectations to the entrepreneur. The entrepreneur might need cash, but just because an investor has the ability to write a check doesn't necessarily mean that he is worthy of being a mentor or guide or, frankly, that he should be listened to at all. So many people have been steered wrong because of money. Having said that, I'll say what I've said a million times at the Stonyfield Farm Entrepreneurs Institute (SFEI): "The bottom, bottom line is always cash."

We joke at SFEI because people come in and think they are challenged by a personnel or a marketing problem, and they might be right, but most of the time they are really confronting a cash problem. In the middle of an institute, somebody might be talking about the challenge of selling a product in another market. While she is talking, something she says will trigger me, and I will start creating a simple cash-flow pro forma on the whiteboard. The entrepreneur usually becomes irritated: "Why is he starting to talk about cash flow when I am talking about a sales or marketing challenge? Why is he going into this stuff about cash flow when I was talking about people management?" Well, the truth is, these challenges are ultimately about cash—specifically, the lack of it.

If you have a company, like mine, where you are raising cash by taking shareholders into your company, that creates its own set of challenges. Although I needed shareholders in order to grow, I didn't want to lose control of my company. I never legally promised any shareholders an exit. Even if I really needed them to invest, when shareholders insisted on this requirement, I didn't accept their money and moved on to other prospects. Even so, I tried to follow my own ethical sense of responsibility to the shareholders who did invest. At one time I had 297 shareholders and whenever any of them needed an exit, I found buyers for that person's shares. Although that was sometimes time-consuming and distracting, the commitment proved to be lifesaving for the company and for me. It was beneficial both because I could get rid of some bad investors that way and because it won me the support of the remaining shareholders. (Some of them had invested when their kids were just born and later faced orthodontic and college bills.)

I was able to help my investors exit because I had a certain amount of control over my cash. You've got to have cash, no matter how great your product is, how great your ideas are, and how great you are. If you don't have a cash-flow pro forma that keeps you focused on never running out and ideally remaining in the black, then shame on you. I say shame on you because that's how people get into bad marriages with investors. And then they or their businesses often fail. How many great people and deals have gone awry because a lack of cash was putting unrealistic pressures on reality? If you don't have that figured out, then it creates a pressure that can force really bad choices.

Respecting Money, Hiring a Professional, and Having a Steady Product

■ JOE, CREATIVE MACHINES

I used to think business was all marketing and nothing else. When I was an undergraduate, I didn't have that much respect for business majors. They were always the ones in the computer lab at midnight printing out a hundred copies of their resume on the laser printer, when the rule was you were supposed to print one copy on the laser and then photocopy the rest on fancy paper. But the business majors were always doing what they wanted. They were the ones who would park in front of the business school without the decal or sticker or whatever you needed in order to park there. I had a certain prejudice about what I thought businesspeople were. It didn't seem like there was any substance to what they were learning and talking about all the time—a whole lot of shells built around no core.

Now, though, I wish I'd had more respect for what they were learning in business school. In order to run a successful business that can make a difference in the world, you need to know double-entry bookkeeping, have an appreciation of cash flow, and grasp some other basics. I've been forced to learn how to do finance, to own my numbers, and to understand cash flow by talking to investors and reading business books. I used to do everything myself. I did the payroll, the budget, the yearly taxes, and so on. When I filed, I figured we didn't really need receipts sorted by month, so I just threw everything in the lower left drawer of my desk. Any paperwork that was sort of official went into that drawer. At the end of the year, I took everything out, put it in a really big clasp envelope, and stuck the envelope on the shelf with a very professional-looking label. I knew it was not a good way to deal with our cash-flow paperwork, but I wanted to spend my time focusing on creating and designing exhibits rather than doing paperwork.

It helps to hire a professional to deal with the aspects of your company (especially those regarding cash flow) that you are not well versed in or don't have the discipline to focus on, and I probably hired my bookkeeper, Paula, later than I should have. When I explained the filing system to her, she said, "That is wrong in so many different ways, I don't know which one to start telling you about." Paula has a really disciplined way of keeping track of our cash flow. Now everything is very well divided. If we need to look up a receipt from a few months ago to see if we are suddenly paying more for welding gases, Paula knows right where to go.

I appreciate having someone I can go to in terms of organizing cash flow and money matters, but I still wake up in the middle of the night worrying about money, especially meeting payroll. We're in a fairly high-risk, high-margin business—at least the way we've been running it. We might make a museum exhibit for $70,000. Maybe we use $10,000 in materials; maybe labor is $20,000. So if all works out, there's a fairly high profit margin. But we can't count on making that profit on every one of our exhibits. We might be late getting an exhibit in, or our exhibits might break down in the institutions we've sent them to. The biggest cost is always time. Employees need time to fool around and try new things, and sometimes those things don't work. Sometimes we sell a $70,000 exhibit, and everything we try doesn't work. We end up spending $80,000 just in labor, and we lose money.

The only way to save yourself from that kind of money problem is to make sure you have a cash reserve that lets you ride out the hard times. You need a product or a service you can always fall back on if some other part of the business fails. For Creative Machines, I realized we had to have some uniform exhibits that we could produce easily, so I've been selling duplicates of the successful exhibits we've developed and placing less of a priority on always doing something new. We also acquired a company that makes ball-machine sculptures. Having these exhibits helps me not wake up in the middle of the night wondering where our next dollar is coming from and whether I will be able to make payroll so my employees can feed their families. We've basically shifted the balance of our work away from custom work and toward duplication and "controlled variation."

A surprising consequence of this shift is that I feel we do a better job with the custom work now. We're not doing as much of it, so we can really take our time. Because we are making money elsewhere, we don't have the same financial pressure bearing down on those projects. I find it more satisfying to do two unusual art pieces or special projects per year and do them really well rather than trying to do twelve and having the quality suffer. When you have someone to manage your cash and when you have a product that gives you a steady cash flow, you can afford to be creative, and your business is ultimately more successful, more innovative, and more fun.

Fear Versus Values

■ MARIE, MS. FOUNDATION AND THE WHITE HOUSE PROJECT

When I go to bed at night worrying about money, when I wake up worrying about something I said to someone about money, when I don't want anyone to bring me the financials so I can get an idea of what I need to do to rise above my money worries, when I am telling myself "This isn't happening, I'm alright, I'm fine, I have enough money," that's when I am in flat denial. That's when I'm essentially lying to myself and not living from my core. We have to be fearless. I am into that word. I'm into it because I feel we're having one of the hardest times we've ever had in our country, and we really have to face it and be fearless. I'm not necessarily fearless myself; I just know we need to be.

People are scared about what is going on. We live in a culture where we're conditioned to numb ourselves when we are afraid. We don't want to move in the direction of our fears. Our allegiance to our integrity and our relationships needs to be bigger than our fears. We can't lose our ability to say to ourselves, "I am representing something that I still believe in." We've got to figure out how we can move through the real fears to deal with the ones that are just anxiety. Some of us transcended being poor, but now we run corporations and nonprofits where we have to deal with that same feeling a lot of the time: "How am I going to pay this month's payroll?" It's like being poor. I was in that place several times, and I don't love it. On the other hand, I was working on issues that are of such importance to women and men in this country, I felt like I just had to get over it and go out and keep doing it.

You have to know when to tell the truth, when to be honest about cash. I had a project that turned out to be the hardest work I'd ever done. I came under a lot of fire because I kept the project going but it was going broke. I had a donor in California I'll never forget. When I sat down with her, she asked where I was financially. I said, "I have to tell you the truth: I'm in a really hard place. I hardly have any money. I know the work is right, but I have no money. I hate to tell you this, but I need your money." She said, "I've been in that place before. I'm going to give you $100,000"—which to me at the time was like a million dollars. Another time, I asked someone for $50,000, and she looked at her check and said, "Oh, I gave you fifty thousand. Did you need more?" And I realized I should have asked for more.

When somebody actually says, "Tell me where you are," I am not going to tell them I don't have any money if I am sitting there with a $500,000 reserve account and three months' rent; I am not going to lie. But if I don't have reserve, it can be difficult to tell people that. I don't want to scare them away. At the same time, sometimes the truth is what can save you. You have to decide when it suits your mission to tell the truth about where you are financially and when the truth need not be revealed.

You always need to know where your money is. You have to have a clear view of it. I'm not a great numbers person, but I could tell you my budget within $100 practically any-time. Some months I'm pretty sure I'm short a certain amount, ($200,000 or whatever), and then I am calculating: "I've got eight donors out there, four of which will come in here, two of which will come in there, so I can do this for the next month. I'm okay. *There's a float.*" At this point I might think, "But I'm not so sure about this next part, so don't bring me the financials and scare me right now. I just need to keep working and not worry about how I am going to get that other money in." Of course, sometimes I know good and well that I am over my head, and I don't look at the financials because I am in complete denial. I just go to bed. That's when I start thinking, "Who am I going to go to to tell the truth?" A couple of months ago, I had to tell the truth about my stress in relation to cash flow, and it was the first time my financial committee really got serious about getting the big money. They kept saying, "Marie can't live like this. We can't let her live like this. This is not good for her." It was really nice to tell the truth and know they stood behind me. You also need people you can call and just laugh about it with.

I never want to lose sight of my values because of cash. If that happens, I know I need to reel myself back in. I've never wanted to do anything entrepreneurial, whether it was launching the Take Our Daughters to Work program or moving the reproductive-rights work to the state level, where I would allow the entrepreneurial side to be weightier than my vision. I want to look beyond the money to the vision and find a way for the two to meet. Money is a symbol for so much: integrity, fear, sickness, truth. It is a resource and a validator. Mostly you have to do three things when you are dealing with money: trust in yourself, trust in your mission, and trust in the balance inherent in the world.

What We Learned

There is no magic answer to solve the tough challenges that arise because of cash problems. But sharing our stories helps. Our thinking can shift when someone like Gary challenges us to recognize that most of our business problems are, at the core, problems with cash. And it is somewhat comforting to know that even at Harvard Business School, the parting wisdom is a handwritten note saying "Cash Is King."

So, now what? How does that help you meet payroll?

It starts with understanding how money comes in and how it flows out. We have seen similar themes running throughout these stories: be frugal, standardize your product in whatever way you can, get the help you need, hold on to your core principles, acknowledge the inherent balancing act between money and values, face your financials when you can, take time out when you can't, and, most importantly, learn to understand your cash flow thoroughly. Below we have distilled our entrepreneurs' advice on owning your numbers. These tips are not a magic wand, but they show one path that might help you deal with the tough stuff.

So that you don't get in the position of having to make really hard trade-offs, you want to do everything in your power to maintain a positive cash flow. Although your company might run out of cash regularly, stretching the dollar always helps. Here are some ways to do this:

- *Negotiate payment terms.* Developing unique relationships with some of your major vendors can be helpful. Lisa's packaging supplier and flour supplier allowed her to pay their bills in sixty days instead of thirty. In the bread business, this cash flow help is critical for a growing company. It meant Lisa's company could get the extra ingredients needed today to fill larger orders tomorrow, but then only had to pay the lower bill from two months ago. Another way to look at this is that the customers paid the bills in thirty days but the bakery had an extra thirty days with that money before the bills came due. For Birkenstock, Margot wasn't able to have more than one supplier. If you have only one supplier, just keep negotiating your terms.

- *Be frugal.* Try to be frugal. After Vermont Bread Company built a new plant in 1988, Lisa bought a secondhand desk for $179 and worked on it her entire career. The staff used to tease her about her frugality because every time she walked past the thermostat in the winter, she turned it down to sixty degrees. In the summertime she turned it up to eighty. As time went on, she realized the company had enough money where the staff didn't have to be cold in the winter and hot in the summer, but for companies that are just starting out, these small changes can make all the difference. With Margot, until Birkenstock was quite large, she used cardboard boxes for wastepaper baskets. Cut expenses any little way you can. The savings can really add up!

- *Standardize your product.* Once Lisa understood her costs, she realized that "the next loaf of bread is free." She knew it wasn't literally free, but the overhead was paid for: the design was done, the truck had more room on it, the batches could be slightly larger, the bill could say 1,001 loaves just as easily as 1,000, and so on. So the profitability of the next loaf was high—as long as she could persuade the salespeople to "sell what we make, in the size we make it, in the package we put it in." Finding a way to do more of what the company was already doing was a key to increasing cash flow. Birkenstock's situation was different: the sandals were a standardized product to begin with and had very few colors and styles. Similar to how Henry Ford said you can have any color car you want as long as it's black, Birkenstock had any color shoe you wanted as long as it was brown. It wasn't until later that the company started offering a variety of styles and colors, and that wreaked a certain amount of havoc on the company's inventory and cash balance.

- *Own your numbers!* See the "Practical Wisdom" section that follows.

■ PRACTICAL TIP
Call Someone You Enjoy Talking to but Whom You Haven't Talked to in a While
Even a quick call to reconnect with an old friend can take your mind off of payroll and sales and cash flow.

■ PRACTICAL TIP
Say "Please" and "Thank You" in as Many Interactions as You Can
In our hurry and stress, we can forget that practicing the value of respect reminds us we are all connected. Creating an environment of respect is a core tenet in most values-driven businesses. So it's great to model it.

Own Your Numbers

Do not turn the page. Come back here for just a minute and let's talk about one of the keys we have found for running our businesses, reducing stress, and making better decisions.

Are you someone whose eyes tend to glaze over when your banker, potential investor, or advisory board member asks you about your gross margin or cash flow? Perhaps you use that pat response "My CFO can answer those questions for you." Owning your numbers is the way to understand your business, make effective decisions, and sleep better at night. To create a healthy, sustainable company, you need to understand certain numbers that tell the story of your business and its vitality. And, yes, you can do it and, no, you do not need an accounting degree or a love of math.

Seven Tips for Owning Your Numbers

Following are some tips to help you own your numbers.

1. *Don't be afraid.* You can do this; it won't take forever. It will provide you with critical information about your business.
2. *There are no stupid questions, and nobody else knows all the answers.* No two businesses are exactly the same, so your critical numbers will be different from other businesses'. Asking questions is the hallmark of a good investigator. You will want to get curious in your quest to understand your business.
3. *Get the right list of what numbers to own.* You don't have to pay attention to all the numbers all the time, but your company has critical "pulse points." Review the list that follows these tips, find someone you can talk with about your company finances, and start learning.

4. *You can do the math if you made it through sixth grade.* Trust us: all the numbers you need to own are the result of basic math—adding, subtracting, multiplying, and dividing.
5. *Learning about your numbers will give you the information you need to make informed decisions.* No explanation is needed: this is the truth!
6. *Owning your numbers is just like learning the basics of a new language.* At first you won't be fluent, and everything will sound unfamiliar, but if you read the translations and speak slowly, over time it will become easier and easier.
7. *Make time every week to look at the numbers.* In just thirty minutes you will know more about your company, what is working, and what isn't.

The Numbers to Own—a Preliminary List

When you master the basics outlined below and know the corresponding numbers every month, you will begin to own your numbers. The goal is to figure out how to get the positive cash flow you need. The information from this puzzle will tell you what to do next.

The Basics of the Income Statement
Find the numbers that correspond to the following:

- Gross margin (How much does it cost to make what you sell? Do certain items have significantly higher or lower gross margins?)
- Total sales by week, month, and year (this year and last year)
- Increase or decrease of sales versus last month and last year

- Returns and chargebacks, totals and as a percentage of sales
- Labor totals (including benefits, FICA, unemployment)
- Labor as a percentage of sales this year versus last year
- General sales and administration as a percentage of sales
- Net income, total and as a percentage of sales this year versus last year
- EBITDA (your net income with interest, taxes, depreciation, and amortization added back in)

Here are a few starting questions about your income statement:

- What surprised you? Why?
- What seems wrong to you?
- What product lines can you reduce without lowering your quality standards?
- On your sales line, what can you sell more of in this economy?
- When you break down your sales versus expenses by product line, which lines are more profitable? Which are less so? Why is that? What can you change?
- What else do you want to know? How can you get those answers?

The Basics of the Balance Sheet
Find the numbers that correspond to the following:

- Cash
- Accounts receivable, total, versus last month, and versus last year

- Inventory, total, versus last month, and versus last year
- Accounts payable, total, versus last month, and versus last year
- Total debt
- Total liabilities
- Total equity

Here are a few starting questions about your balance sheet:

- How are you using your cash? Can you bring it in sooner and keep it longer?
- How long (in days) does it take to get your money in the door (your accounts receivable)?
- How long (in days) does it take you to pay your bills (your accounts payable)?
- How long (in days) does your inventory last?
- Can you see ways to increase or decrease the above indicators to help with your cash flow?
- What is your total debt divided by your total equity (your debt-to-worth ratio)?

*The Basics of Key Performance Measures for
Your Company*
Performance measures are different for every company, so spend some time figuring out what numbers are key to your business. Figure out your best answer, measure that, and keep an open mind for a better measure to appear over time (and know it is okay to change it).

Some of the measures we have used in our companies are the following:

- Percentage of capacity
- Sales per employee

- Cost per unit of delivery (product, hours, dollars)
- Sales per salesperson per week
- Pounds of bread per person per hour
- Quality measurement (i.e., unsalable product, number of complaints)

What Next?

Given what you have learned about your numbers, what three performance measures matter most? And from those things, what actions will you take?

Performance Measures	Actions
1. _____	_____
2. _____	_____
3. _____	_____

Okay, now breathe—and reread this section tomorrow, after you have had a cup of coffee and some time to spend with the information. Every day it will make more sense. The numbers are like a puzzle to be solved. Understanding the puzzle will help you be a better leader for your company.

Coping with everyday stressors

This chapter could also be titled "This Chaos Is Normal" or "The Tough Stuff Never Ends—It Just Changes." Nothing is ever smooth in business. Things rarely run exactly as they should without challenges that keep you up at night. You run out of cash, you lose a big customer, a key employee threatens to quit, or you have to deal with brutal competition. You might have a product crisis or family complications that impact your productivity at work: a sick kid, problems with your partner, a dying parent. Sometimes you think that if you can just get through *this* tough stuff, you will get a break. That almost never happens. Each new leap you take feels like the same height as the last huge leap, and leaps you used to think were big don't seem so big in the rearview mirror. Now you wish you had a "small" problem like the one before, a problem you have already learned how to deal with.

In this chapter you will read some stories about how entrepreneurs got through their everyday stressors, large and small, and lived to tell about them. These entrepreneurs found help, learned to take care of themselves, and realized that reflecting on the stressors helped them grow their businesses. Lisa talks about using a calm, steady approach to implement change at

Vermont Bread Company. Margot discusses the importance of taking action rather than assigning blame during a crisis. Joe explains the challenges of finding a balance between hiring and not hiring and between controlling your employees and giving them autonomy. And Carol Berry of Putney Pasta reveals her story about a company tragedy, giving us the confidence that even the worst nightmare can be weathered with some patience and time.

If you sometimes feel that you are at the end of your rope and you need to know that other people get stressed, too, here's the chapter for you. Hopefully the practical tips at the end will give you calming antidotes for those times when you feel frayed and spent.

Mantras, Patience, and Taking Care of *You*

■ LISA

Before I got into the bread business, I never even thought about how food got to the supermarket. In truth, it's very complicated. It's an everyday stressor! There is always something to worry about and be stressed about. For instance, one spring, the lab we worked with sent me enriched-flour values for my labels rather than the unenriched-flour values I needed. So, on a line of five products, all my vitamin counts were wrong. The Food and Drug Administration told me to pull the mislabeled products off the market and relabel them. Another rainy spring, the mold spore count in the Northeast was the highest it had ever been, and our product was getting moldy before the date marked on the package. I've faced all sorts of other stressors I couldn't have imagined before I started Vermont Bread Company.

As I think about these stresses and what helped us day to day, I realize that the sayings we repeated regularly and the rules that became chants helped us through some of our most difficult times. "The bread will go out" is a good example. This phrase became our overarching mantra. In the bread business, the basic saying has to be *"The bread will go out"* because today's bread has to be delivered today to fill the empty space on the supermarket shelf. The balance sheet for a bake-to-order wholesale bread factory does not have a "finished goods inventory" category.

It's a crazy business model if you think about it: all the bread must be baked, sliced, bagged, and put on tractor-trailers to go to warehouses. It has to be separated into routes, picked up by drivers in bread trucks, and delivered to every store we service by 10:00 a.m., five days a week. This environment has little room for error, so it can be very stressful, especially if machines break down or remakes are needed to replace poor-quality products. "The bread will go out" was the answer whenever a machine broke down: I would ask the engineer how it was going and his first response was always "The bread *will* go out." This meant, for the last shift of the cycle, if the orders were not complete, nobody even thought about going home. It meant if we were short-staffed, any one of us would fill in for a production worker. That led to another of our sayings: "It's *all* my job." It was not an accounting clerk's responsibility to work at the oven every day, but if asked, the answer always needed to be yes. Another saying we had was "We and ours, not me and mine." It reflected an attitude of teamwork that was important in our culture.

In order to deal effectively with everyday stressors, we also tried to instill the clear value of respect in our dealings with one another. One of our strict rules was "Thou shall not yell, swear, or name-call in the workplace." And the companion rule was "If you are feeling close to doing any of those things, go outside immediately and walk around the building as quickly as you can." When the morale of our office staff was slipping and I noticed more irritation in people's voices, more sighing, and more rolling of the eyes, I started posting "If you are not having a good day . . . Fake It." For the most part, these rules were honored and repeated, and many new hires told me they had never been so well treated, so welcomed, and so respected by any other manufacturing company they worked in.

With everyday stressors, a calm, patient approach usually worked. Sometimes, I was virtually alone in my rules and mantras, saying them over and over again and hoping that by doing this I could implement change. It could make me feel lonely and futile, but if I used a steady, unflustered approach, change would eventually happen. For example, early on we had to switch from allowing hats for headwear in the production areas to requiring the more professional and sanitary use of hairnets. This change was met by surprising resistance from our production workers. Every morning I would walk out onto the production floor and calmly say again and again, "You have to wear a hairnet." A couple of hours later I would say to the next group coming on shift, "You have to wear a hairnet." I did not raise my voice or use an irritated tone. Finally, the change happened. A small group gave in, and they started to help with the chant. Then more people joined until we all had hairnets on our heads. Then I began again: "The hairnet needs to cover all the hair on your head to be effective, even if your bangs look better hanging out in front."

Another stressor at Vermont Bread Company was the issue of safety. Because we were working in manufacturing, we needed to be really aware of safety and backup plans at all times. At the bakery, we used to have a machine called an intermediate proofer that was ten feet tall, held over three hundred baskets of bread, and was driven by a chain as thick as a belt. The chain wound around a metal sprocket about as large as a dinner plate. Removable safety guards prevented anything from getting caught in the machinery. Time and time again I issued safety warnings and repeated the mantra "Do not take the guards off. Do not run the machine without the guards. Do not bypass the guard system." My workers used to take the guards off anyway. When they were in the middle of a production run and moving quickly, the guards could make the bread loaves jam, so some of the workers figured out how to bypass them. Without the guards, the workers could quickly and easily reach into the machine to clear out the loaves that were piling up. Then one long-term employee put his hand in there and got distracted, and the chain came up around his arm. Fortunately, the machine stopped because of a torque limiter my partner had installed after watching the workers take the guards off so many times despite repeated warnings.

This incident was a really good lesson that in order to deal with everyday stressors, you can't just blindly plow forward. Mantras like "Do not bypass the guard system" are good ones, but you must be aware of what is really going on. This was true, too, with mantras like "The bread will go out." I remember one Sunday morning I stopped by to check on a new high-speed machine that sliced, bagged, and put a plastic closure lock on the bread. Nothing was going right. More bread was being destroyed than packaged. We were running behind schedule. People were trying to hurry. The bins that held the rejects were overflowing. The trucks were held up leaving the bakery and tempers were running shorter by the minute. The runners were having a difficult time sliding the full stacks of baskets across the floor because of the piles of waste bread. I didn't just say, "The bread will go out"; I assessed the situation and acted accordingly. Even though we were running really late, I shut down the line, grabbed a broom, and had everyone join me in cleaning up the packaging room. People grumbled, shook their heads, and rolled their eyes, but they cleaned. Within thirty minutes we were back up and running. Everyone's mood had lightened. There were smiles and laughter. We got it finished at a much faster rate than we had been working at. And the bread *did* go out!

Chanting mantras in the workplace and using a calm, steady approach to implement change were two of the ways I dealt with everyday stressors while running a socially responsible business. When I was most stressed at Vermont Bread Company, though, I needed to remember why I was in business in the first place, and I would stand at the oven and watch the loaves come out and go through a depanner. In that spot in the plant, a person can really get connected to the product. It was always a place I would go to calm down. I considered it a meditation.

Communication—the Path of Least Resistance and a Weekend Away

■ MARGOT

One thing I can say about stressors is, they'll show up every day in one form or another. A good thing to remember while you are going through them is that there is almost always an inherent lesson in a stressor. Finding the lesson can be the silver lining in the cloud; however, often you have to look for it. For example, one year we had just started shipping our spring sandals and were eagerly expecting another forty-foot container, holding twelve thousand pairs of sandals. When it pulled into our parking lot, we quickly became dismayed as we began to unload the merchandise and discovered that somewhere along the way, the container had sprung a leak and had sat in the rain. Many of the sandals were soaking wet, and a few already showed signs of mildew. We called our insurance agent, who said to let everything sit until someone came to assess the damage. We had no time to find the culprit—more shoes would get ruined. Instead, we needed to take immediate action and rescue as many shoes as possible. We took photographs of the mess to establish our claim and went back to work. Quite a few sandals could be salvaged, but the shoeboxes were a total loss. Our manufacturer in Germany sent thousands of replacement boxes and original tissue paper on the next airplane. Luckily the shoeboxes were collapsible for easy stacking; otherwise, getting them quickly would have been almost impossible.

That day we recognized that sometimes stressors can have the benefit of promoting interdependence, developing understanding, and enhancing communication and cooperation between departments. Because of our dire emergency, all the workers were pressed into service, no matter what department they were from. We organized shifts to unpack and dry shoes. When the new boxes arrived, we reboxed and relabeled everything. It was a monumental effort, but we rescued the season. The crisis connected people who had never spoken with one another before. Working side by side on a rather mundane task made us realize that every job was important and necessary for the good of the whole. When we were small, this particular issue had never been a problem because most people worked in more than one department and wore more than one hat. But once we had gotten to a certain size, that changed and some "silo thinking" had set in. This crisis helped to change that.

You can learn just as much from long-term stressors as you can from acute crises. Other stressors popped up that were not so immediate but affected the company on a day-to-day basis. For instance, some workers had a hard time with certain parts of their jobs. I wanted to keep the employees, yet it was a constant struggle to figure out how to get around their apparent weaknesses. An example of this was a young woman working in marketing. She didn't like the flowery speech the other people in her department used. She preferred to "tell it like it is," and this did not endear her to the rest of the team. She was smart and a good worker, and I didn't want to lose her, so I asked if she liked numbers. She loved numbers, so we put her into accounting. With numbers you have to tell the truth—you have to tell it like it is. She worked out wonderfully! Thinking creatively and outside the box could help tremendously when we had a long-term stressor we were trying to solve.

Sometimes your stressor is that you have people you can't deal with at all and you have to fire them. But sometimes you can't even do that! One man who worked for us was getting very cocky and wasn't good for morale. I had just gotten up my nerve to fire him when he went on a joyride on his new motorcycle and had a bad accident. Of course, I couldn't fire him then. His injuries weren't bad enough that he could go on disability, so I had to drag him along for another six months or so so that he could heal and be ready to look for another job. That was a terrible situation for which there was no creative solution.

How do you prepare for everyday stressors, and what do you do when you can't get rid of them? Usually the stressors were nothing that a nice weekend away in the country couldn't fix, but I also liked to sing rousing songs at the top of my voice while driving to work every morning. Nobody could hear whether I was off-key, nobody could interrupt my pleasure, and singing put me in the right frame of mind for the challenges that lay ahead.

Getting and Keeping Good Employees

■ JOE, CREATIVE MACHINES

One of my stressors when I first started came from the fact that I wasn't running my business like a franchise. Some pretty good business books out right now are geared toward how to run your business like a franchise. They tell you to create jobs so the intelligence is in the system rather than the people. It's sort of like making McDonald's french fries: you don't even time it yourself—the fryer beeps when you need to do this, it beeps when you need to do that, it beeps when you need to put the salt on, it beeps when you need to put a new batch in. I don't really think that all your jobs have to be "beep jobs," but I didn't have *any* beep jobs at Creative Machines, and I had to learn the hard way that you need a mix of beep jobs and creative jobs. I didn't think my employees would appreciate this, but actually they did. Back when I had only one or two employees, I made the mistake of thinking they wanted what I wanted. I was trying to make a work environment for a dozen mini-mes, so I gave them a zillion choices of what to work on, and I came up with something new to do every day. However, my employees were frustrated. They didn't want a zillion choices and something new to do every day. They wanted to come to work in the morning, have a clear plan of what they were going to do, and accomplish it. They wanted to take home their paychecks and be with their families on the weekends and then come in on Monday to do it all over again.

As with any challenge, I learned a lot from that. More than creative thinkers, I needed flexible thinkers: people who could deal with new situations, people who not only were creative but knew how to manage creativity. It took me a while to hire the group I have now. Now when I get applications from people who say, "I would love this job," and they proceed to tell me how the job would help them express their creativity, I know I have to be careful. I've learned that the reason for hiring people is not to fulfill their own creative life journeys. That's their responsibility. Making public art and museum exhibits seems attractive to a lot of people, and some people want to work for us so badly they overlook the reasons working here is not an ideal job. Over the years I've learned to devote a good portion of job advertisements and interviews to the bad parts of the job. I'd rather have people start with a balanced view rather than deciding it's not for them a few years down the road.

Not hiring people has also added to my stress along the way. As my business grew, it always seemed easier to just do the extra work myself rather than to train the next person. A lot of times I was working in panic mode to get work done, and it felt quicker to put off hiring someone rather than to have unproductive time when I was putting an ad in the paper, interviewing, and then training. But hiring was essential to making the business move, and it alleviated everyday stress in the long run.

Hiring people with good judgment and then helping them develop that judgment is a big part of my everyday challenge. It takes good listening, good intuition, and a little luck. What we do is semicustom, so I need people who can think on their feet and have good judgment. They need to be able to tell the difference between times when a project is good as it is and will get only marginally better with an increase in work and times when they really do need to work on the project more. If they are making a complicated exhibit with a lot of moving parts, they have to know in what order to put the pieces together. They have to think about what social environment the exhibit is going into and ask themselves if it will need to be serviced regularly, whether anyone should be able to get into the cabinet with just a screwdriver, or if it would be better to limit access to those with a key. Some of those are mechanical questions, but some of them are judgment questions.

I have created stress by letting employees work too independently, by not having them talk aloud about these choices. It's not that they aren't smart enough to work independently, but when an employee doesn't have someone to bounce an idea off of, he can make mistakes. If he's not forced to articulate something, if he works in a vacuum, he can make bad choices. For instance, one employee made a water exhibit using regular steel instead of stainless steel, which caused warranty problems down the road. It's the sort of mistake he shouldn't have made. He seemed very independent—he didn't want to collaborate or talk about what he did, so I left him alone. In a way, it was my mistake for allowing him to work too independently. I didn't give him an opportunity to articulate what he was doing. Now I try to have people work in teams because you think differently if you say things aloud. Your brain is activated in a different way when you speak aloud. When you are forced to say something like "Should we use this bolt here?" you think about the task again in a way that you wouldn't if you were working alone. Being an employer is sort of like being a psychologist and figuring out how people do their best work.

What's helped me with the stress? There are all sorts of formal techniques for stress management, but I think a lot of people just discover what works best for them, and that's what I've done. I've used a lot of visualization techniques and ways of calming myself to take the pressure off. Breathing and stretching work best to calm and focus me. Then in my mind I start from square one, and I think, "How stressed can I be? I'm not starving. There are no immediate physical threats to my life and limb or to my family. We're not in imminent danger of being killed. Anything else can be worked out." A lot of stress is psychological, so I find ways to cool off and ask myself, "What do I really have to do to solve the problem? Let's imagine that I'm going to succeed. What are the steps I need to take to get there?" Rather than try to think of the most creative solution, I try to think of the simplest, dumbest thing I could do. I might think, "Well, I could borrow the money I need from this source because we have a line of credit there. That's a solution I don't necessarily want to pursue, but it's a fallback." Then that suddenly frees me up, and I am able to see other, better solutions. Considering the obvious makes me less driven to find the really cool answer, but I've learned that psychologically, it makes it easier to let go in my thinking in order to find a more clever solution.

My business isn't me, even if it feels like it is on some days. If the business fails, I'll find something else to do. I'll start all over again and—who knows?—it might be an even better life. I can't imagine that now—I love what I do—but you have to be ready to do the best you can and then brace yourself for what life brings you.

Weathering a Company Tragedy

■ **CAROL, PUTNEY PASTA**

I had more than what most people would call an everyday stressor, though the threat of a similar incident is a stress that many business owners hold onto every day. When you run a plant and you work around big machines every day, you sometimes forget how dangerous they are. You forget that someone could die in the blink of an eye. When it actually happens, it is one of the most horrible things that a business owner can imagine. Having something happen to someone at your plant is similar to when something happens to a member of your family for whom you are responsible. I remember I was leading my stepson on a horse; this was maybe thirty years ago, but I still remember it very clearly. He just kind of slid off onto the ground. He broke his arm. Some friends were there, and we all found ways to feel guilty, to blame ourselves.

In manufacturing, unless the plant is closed, you are never absolved from responsibility, and that can be stressful. You could be halfway around the world, but the people at your company still have to be able to reach you by phone. I had gone on vacation the day before the accident at my plant happened. I was visiting my mother in Las Vegas, and from there I planned to go to California. I had just woken up the morning after I arrived at my mother's when I got a call from the town manager. She said, "Bruce just died in your equipment." I said, "No. No way." I couldn't believe it. The town manager was a friend of mine, and when the call came into the town office, she had followed the fire trucks to my plant. I was on a plane by that afternoon, and I cried all the way back. I still feel the heartache and the tears today as I write about this.

In order to get through stress like that, you have to find ways not to beat yourself up, and you have to have really good friends who won't back down when the going gets tough. After the accident happened, I was with my employees. We were all reeling from the shock and the grief. At the same time, I had to deal with brutality in the press, a public whipping in the media, and deep humiliation. All I wanted to do was give myself to my employees and my grief. I had to isolate myself for a few days. At the time, Lisa Lorimer said to me, "It could just as easily have happened in my bread plant." Those words meant more to me than anything else I heard during that time. Someone actually recognized that we didn't do something god-awful. We ran a really nice plant and in any plant you can find places that could do a lot of harm. I weathered the storm and got back as soon as I could, but I couldn't have done it without my friends. They were wonderful. Their support was terrific. They stood beside me the whole time. That's how I got through my grief.

What We Learned

You are not the only one who sometimes feels like your company is a house of cards. The stressors are real, they are tough, and they don't ever end. Over time, they may change, and the tasks that used to be difficult may seem easier, but no company runs smoothly all the time. Our entrepreneurs' stories offer some ideas for helping you get through the stresses that inevitably come your way:

- *Make sure your mantras are on target with your business goals and values.* What are the mantras in your company? Have they shifted over the years? Do they need to shift now? Use them with patience and quietude to make the change you want to see.

- *Find the place in your company that reminds you of your core mission.* Be sure to continually make a connection to the passion you have for your work. Lisa often went to a place where she could watch the bread come out of the oven. Where is this place for you? Remember to visit there when the everyday stressors pile up.

- *Read the "What We Learned" sections and "Practical Tips" sections at the end of these chapters.* The coping strategies that have helped us deal with stressors are collected in the tips at the end of each chapter. These tips provide actions you can take to create some quiet space so that you can be reflective rather than reactive. For instance, one of the suggestions is to create an advisory board so you have a place where you can hit the pause button and get some help working on your business, rather than the business working on you. Even if some of these tips sound hokey at first, try them.

Everyday stressors will always be there, but by taking care of yourself and finding ways to release tension, you can be steadier in the face of any challenge.

■ PRACTICAL TIP
Use Your Commute Time to Change Your Attitude About the Everyday Stressors
Margot liked to use her commute to sing rousing songs at the top of her voice: "Nobody could hear whether I was off-key and nobody could interrupt my pleasure. It put me in the right frame of mind for the challenges that lay ahead in my day."

■ PRACTICAL TIP
Try to Find the Simplest, Dumbest Answer First
Like Joe, you might try to think of the simplest answer rather than the most complicated one when you have a problem. This way of thinking can free you up to find more creative solutions. Having a "fallback" plan can take some of the stress away and allow you to think more clearly. Don't let your ego or your pride get involved when thinking of these "easy" solutions; just make sure you have one last resort you can go to if all else fails.

Learning to trust yourself

Idealism, vision, and gut-trusting can help you plunge forward in pursuit of your dreams. We have all heard about the American icon: the entrepreneur. He has wild stories about what it was like in the "old days" when he started his now-successful company. A lot of times he will begin his tale with "If I knew then what I know now, I never would have begun." He might talk about how much he believed in his product and how he went against all the odds to make it happen. But it's hard to hold on to that kind of optimism and self-reliance in the face of industry naysayers. You might also have to face your own feeling that you should be doing one thing when your intuition is actually leading you to do something else.

This chapter is about learning to trust that intuition. It is about knowing when to move ahead with your core values. It is about finding the balance between being an innovative rule-breaker and making it in the mainstream. In Lisa's case, everyone told her the product she believed in would fail, yet she continued to trust her mission and open doors for the company to grow. Margot felt she was being compromised at a trade show, and she broke industry rules by slipping out the fire escape, only to find that success followed her home. Gary learned that trusting in yourself and acting impulsively were not the same thing. Carol learned that her love of risk that she inherited from her father did not mean she had to give up her belief in loyalty. And Tom Raffio of Northeast Delta Dental figured out how to stay true to his values by focusing on sufficiency rather than greed.

These stories are about times when entrepreneurs have put self-doubt aside and hoped that their values systems would lead them where they needed to be. Sometimes our intuitive sense can be better than all the business know-how in the world.

One Loaf at a Time

■ **LISA**

When I think back to our early days and the crazy things we did, I cringe. But I know if we had listened to the experts, we never would have succeeded. I didn't actually go to Harvard Business School until I had been in business for many years. In the early years, I didn't know anything except that I believed in my product and I needed to take each decision one at a time. Everyone in the industry kept telling us it was not possible to make and sell all-natural bread: the dough would be too stiff for the mixers, the loaf would be too dense to be sliced, the bread would mold on the supermarket shelves, and so on. But we were bullheaded about it. We didn't want to make bread with the chemicals people were telling us about, so we started by selling to local stores and farmers' markets.

Even though the experts told us it could not be done, we did find our way onto the supermarket shelves because our bread was unique, it tasted great, and, luckily, we were located in a vacation destination. Very early on, a vice president at one of the largest supermarket chains in the Northeast was on vacation in Vermont and bought our bread at a local farmers' market. He called to talk about having us supply his chain's

stores. We said, "Sure, we can meet you." In those days everyone did everything. In the early morning hours, we baked the
bread, we packaged it, and we made the deliveries. When we
came back, we cleaned the bakery and paid bills. At the end of
one of those days we went to see the vice president of this huge
supermarket chain. He told us he wanted to put our product in
3 test stores. We said, "Great! But you are this huge company,
and we are this little bakery. We've been learning about cash
flow, and if you take thirty days to pay your bill, you will put
us out of business." He laughed and said, "No problem—we
will pay you cash." So we delivered to each store's back door,
took out our returns, stocked the shelf, got the invoice signed,
went to the courtesy booth, and received our cash. Fifteen
years later we were servicing all of the stores and starting a
private label program with the chain. One day our driver came
to us and said he no longer felt safe walking around with all of
that money in his pocket. I called the buyer and said, "Thanks
for all your help in the early days, but you don't have to pay
us cash now. We can bill those 3 original stores along with the
other 150."

As we grew quickly and expanded our territory, my intuition told me I didn't know enough to run the business alone. I
needed help. But I was afraid. We didn't have a lot of money, and
I was worried about our cash flow. I had hired a consultant to
come in weekly to help us with correcting our recipes for larger
batches. He identified machines that could make the work easier, standardized our production procedures, trained our people
to be better bakers, and formulated new products. We needed
him or someone like him to be on staff full-time. Even though
intuitively I knew this, I was still nervous about spending that
kind of money. Finally, I followed my instincts and hired him.
He was a general manager with twenty-seven years of industry
experience. It was one of my first strategic hires.

Even though my intuition told me to hire him, I had been worried about adding that level of salary to the company, but one decision he made in the first week—to change the type of yeast we used—saved the company two times his yearly salary and expenses. When he came into our company, he was constantly surprised. He still says he can't believe we grew to be the largest natural bakery east of the Mississippi, and not one person in the company knew how to bake. He used to leave little notes everywhere saying "Lisa, you *bake* bread you don't *cook* it" because we all used to say "*cook* the bread."

Learning to trust yourself doesn't always mean listening to the industry experts and knowing everything. When I started out, I might not have known much, but I *did* know how to listen to my intuition, and I knew we had a good product I wanted to stand behind. Our bread was made without chemicals and without preservatives. It was healthy and it made great toast. It was different (and I thought better) than anything else that was being sold in stores. I knew that if I protected the core value—healthy bread that was different—then I had a real story to tell. And it was the story that got us shelf space in stores. It was a story of a new type of product that expressed our values. It tasted great and provided good jobs for all of us working at the bakery. Everything else we had to figure out— one piece at a time, one decision at a time, one step at a time, one loaf at a time.

The More You Hold On, the Less You'll Have

■ MARGOT

When I started Birkenstock, I was not fixed on traditional ways of running a company. I had no preconceived ideas of what was correct, so I was able to listen to what was happening in the world and follow my own instincts. I was not merely concentrating on a bottom line; I was concentrating on spreading the word about Birkenstock, one pair of shoes at a time. The first ten years of running Birkenstock, I kept thinking that somebody else with this opportunity would have done a better job. I hadn't gone to business school yet, and I hadn't really learned how to do things right. But as the years went by, it began to dawn on me that I was precisely the right person in the right place at the right time. Someone else who knew the supposed "right way" would have done things according to business books and probably wouldn't have understood the spirit of Birkenstock that ultimately sold the shoes.

An early experience reinforced my belief that following my intuition and trusting myself might be one of the best skills available to me. In 1972 we were still selling exclusively to health-food stores. I saw how limited this was and decided it was time to branch out and try a shoe show again. In those days the Western Shoe Retailers Association held shows in a small two-story hotel near the San Francisco airport. We showed the shoes right there in a hotel room on the bed. Since I was a newcomer to the show, I was put on the second floor at the end of the hall. It was the loneliest time I've ever had at a show—the only people who came in were other salesmen, and one even tried to get fresh with me. I figured the show wasn't working and I wanted to leave. It was Sunday; the show lasted two more days; unless we stayed until the end, we wouldn't be allowed to ever show there again. Well, I decided to follow my own intuition, and I packed up everything and fled by the fire escape. I didn't care if I ever showed there again. I just wanted to get home. I kept thinking that the very next morning I could be back in the office being productive.

As it turned out, it was good that I followed my instinct to go to the show, but it was also fine that I followed my intuition to leave. That "bad" show gave us one contact that would be pivotal to our development and the starting point of our future success. This is what happened: A young man riding the escalator at the hotel overheard someone say, "Did you see anything new at this show?" The other person answered, "Not really. Only those Birkenstock sandals, and they looked weird!" This intrigued the eavesdropper, but by the time he looked us up in the directory, I had already gone. After the show was over, he came to our office and bought twelve pairs of sandals. He and his brother had a gift shop in Carmel, where they sold handcrafted leather bags, belts, jewelry, and other artistic goods. After about six months, the older brother remarked that the sandals didn't pay off. The eavesdropper convinced him they just didn't have enough of them—those few pairs did not create a big impact. He visited us again and bought a whole wall full of sandals. This really kicked off their business, and two years later they decided to start a separate store specializing only in Birkenstocks.

Life acts in surprising ways. The disastrous shoe show turned out to be a great success after all. I learned not to be too quick to judge failed efforts and taught my people to do the same. Who knows what seeds might be sown and when they might sprout and bear fruit?

Experiences like these taught me not to despair when situations don't work out as first envisioned. They taught me to just keep following my own intuition. I think the necessity of trusting myself came from my experience during the war. With all the destruction I saw as a child, I realized that nothing was permanent. I saw fortunes disappear overnight. Some people survived their losses, and some didn't. That's why I tried not to hang on to things. I hoped things I cared about *would* last, but I didn't count on it. Instead, I trusted my own sense that most situations wouldn't turn out exactly the way they were planned. I couldn't necessarily count on the outcome, so I would just do the best I could every day and take it from there. It might not be optimal, but I came to believe that if I figured out how to adapt and adjust, usually everything turned out to be workable. My biggest truth was this: *the more you hold on, the less you'll have.*

The thing that did stay with me throughout the years was my belief in the Birkenstock product. I actually had more trust in the product than I had in myself. It turned out that having faith in our product was exactly what was needed at the time. Young people wanted to look different from their mothers. They wanted to earn their living differently from their fathers. They wanted to do something meaningful. They did not want to give up their values for a paycheck. One of these young people was a student in Seattle. She convinced a friend who owned a health-food store to give her a little space to sell the sandals. Just a few hours a week, she waited for customers while doing her schoolwork. That situation became cumbersome after a while: people trying on shoes always created a mess, and her friend did not appreciate it. The girl coaxed her father into giving her some money to open her own store. Her father wanted assurance that she was not going to waste his money, so I sent her a letter stating that if the store didn't work out, I would take back her original order and refund the money. She has that letter framed on the wall of her store over thirty years later.

Because I believed in the product and in the spirit of the brand, I was willing to take a chance with unproven concepts and inexperienced retailers. I trusted that the sellers loved the product like I did and could relate this love to consumers. Some of these early folks are still in business many years later. By selling something they believed in, they built a life for themselves, put their kids through college, and felt good about how they were making a living.

Someone who knew how to do things "right" probably would have looked only at the bottom line from the beginning and would not have been able to nurture Birkenstock into what it became over the years. I didn't create a franchise system because I didn't like the rules and regulations connected with that. We did not have a strategic plan to create stores. Instead, people searched us out. They came for different reasons, and each had different needs. They were all individuals, living in various communities all over the country, so I couldn't see tying them down to cookie-cutter designs and making the stores look alike everywhere. I wanted the sellers to be able to express their individuality. We had about two hundred stores that carried the name "Birkenstock" over their doors. We were the envy of the trade. People were asking how such inexperienced folks pulled this off. Several other comfort-shoe brands tried to emulate us. They did it "right," the way it "should" be done—with marketing and money—but it didn't work out for them. We never rushed to grow too quickly. We never held on too tight. This approach gave the brand an enduring quality.

Warped Genes and the Internal Wrestling Match

■ GARY, STONYFIELD FARM

There are two very important things in terms of starting a business, and neither one of them is knowledge. The first is determination. Determination is one of the most undervalued attributes for an entrepreneur, and it can make up for a lot of other things that you may lack. The second attribute is a belief in yourself. When people are starting businesses, I always counsel them that it's okay not to know everything. Some of the world's greatest feats have been accomplished by people not smart enough to know those feats were impossible. Sometimes the less you know, the better. When embarking

on the road to being an entrepreneur, anybody who thinks it's going to be easy is (a) in for a big surprise and (b) wrong. It's *never* easy. It's never *been* easy. If it isn't torturous, you are probably not going to be successful. A certain amount of transformation will probably happen as your business grows. You will have to let go of certain things, like comfort and sleep, in order to gain new things: success, wisdom, and experience. But you don't always know this at first, and that's actually good. I can take no credit for going into my own business knowing what the answers were going to be or what it would be like. None at all. It was an absolute result of holding my nose and jumping in, deciding to swim with the sharks and having them turn into dolphins, or whatever the analogy would be.

But there is a big difference between acting confidently and actually trusting deeply in yourself. The latter took me a while to understand. I would act with confidence, leaping off planks and sailing off cliffs, but I learned that wasn't necessarily trusting myself. Trusting yourself means you bring some discipline to the process and you don't just go on your gut. All good entrepreneurs and leaders have an internal wrestling match between intuition and pragmatics. They also know when to stop wrestling and get on with it. It's a balance, and finding that balance can be difficult.

To some extent, I think entrepreneurs seek to be unbalanced. It's in our natures, our warped genes. I always used to stand up at Social Venture Network conferences, put up my hand, and say, "My name is Gary, and I'm totally out of balance." In order to find this balance that might not be inherent to my nature, I go through a mental checklist that aligns with my value system, and I almost always double-check with my wife before I make a decision. This is part of how I have developed trust in myself that I will make good choices. My wife is not an entrepreneur, and she is completely risk averse (except that she married me, which was risky). She is happy to take a loss and move on. She has no problem saying "Okay, that was a dead end. Tomorrow's another day," whereas, I don't like the idea of limits, I don't like putting up the white flag—it's just not my way. I don't like the word "no" very much, but that's probably true of all entrepreneurs. To find some sort of balance, where balance might be lacking, I have to check in with my wife and hear her commentary. She and I disagree on almost everything when it comes to business. I can reject her suggestions, but it's on my checklist to run everything by her. I still rely heavily on my gut after going through the checklist, but I always make myself go through that process first, at least with the important decisions.

So knowing how to trust yourself is really about balance: the balance between going with your gut feeling and having the discipline to think about what makes sense, the balance between knowing when to trudge through and when to cut your losses and move on, the balance between making snap decisions and delaying too long, and the balance between trying to please everyone and just getting the job done. It starts with trusting yourself and having determination. It also starts with a great product you can believe in.

Embracing the Bumpy Roads of Business and the Risk Fix

■ **CAROL, PUTNEY PASTA**

In order to know how to trust yourself, you first have to know yourself. Knowing yourself starts with understanding where you come from and how your values developed. I am from a family of six kids, so all of us differentiated ourselves to be unique. It was well known in my family that I was my father's favorite. I was the tough one, physically and emotionally, which helped me tremendously when I went into business later on. I was tough because of where I fell in the pecking order; I was number four. I have an older sister who was pretty difficult. My mother said she wanted to be an only child, but when five more kids came on the scene, she lost her place in the family, especially since I was daddy's little girl. I had to be tough to deal with her, and I also had to be tough to be the spokesperson for the younger ones. I had two little sisters, and I was their protector. My younger sisters would come to me and say, "Ask Dad if I can do this or that," and he was not an easy guy at all. Being the protector became my role in business when I was dealing with employees as the president of my company.

I learned a lot from my father in terms of what I valued and did not value about business. He was a true entrepreneur and a very bright guy. He went to the Wharton School of Business, and when he finished school, he bought a few Army/Navy surplus shops in Rhode Island. He then joined the Navy. Before he went off to war he told my mother to run the shops—not that she's a businesswoman; she just did whatever had to be done. After the war, he bought and developed an industrial park where boats had been built during the war. He always liked to be the first. He had the first bowling lane, the first amusement park, and the first trampoline center in Rhode Island. He also had a beautiful marina right on Narragansett Bay. He built a hotel that he sold to Hilton. I watched him reinvent himself with each new business. I loved being involved in his businesses from the time I was a little girl. Summers I didn't want to go to camp, I wanted to work for my father. I worked at the amusement park one summer and at the restaurant another summer and on down the line. I loved being part of his businesses. But I also saw that he was never satisfied. He was restless. It was never enough.

My father had his first major heart attack at thirty-eight years old. When he was forty-six the doctor said to him, "If you don't quit smoking and lose weight, you'll be dead in five years." Almost five years to the day, he was dead. He was semi-retired by then, had moved to Florida, and had gotten involved in racehorses. He died at the racetrack. Sometimes I wish he were still alive today, but other times I'm glad he isn't because I'm not sure he would be supportive of me. I loved my father's entrepreneurial spirit, yet I did not want to keep reinventing myself. I had a need for speed, but I learned that I was not quite the risk taker he was. I wanted a certain amount of continuity in my life. For me, I can get my risk fix at the racetrack. I went to racing school in Colorado, and I love racing cars.

If you know yourself and learn to embrace your lineage and channel your attributes and strengths, you can do really well at what you choose to do. The core values I learned growing up were staying tough through hard times, being a protector and a spokesperson, and enjoying the speed of business while remaining committed to one company. I trusted in those values, and they led me through my time with Putney Pasta. I never got bored there. I liked being familiar with something, protecting my employees, staying tough through the bumpy times. I was lucky—courage and strong-heartedness were the stock of my family. It's in my father, it's in me, and it's in three out of six of us siblings, who are strong, good businesspeople. We do well in the tumult of business. We don't mind chaos.

Taking a Hit and Remaining Happy

■ TOM, NORTHEAST DELTA DENTAL

For me, learning to trust yourself means adhering to your values. I have always tried to be value driven. Before I came to Northeast Delta Dental, I was the number-two person at Delta

Dental of Massachusetts. At the beginning, the company was shaky in terms of if it would succeed. It was a start-up company then, but by the time I left it was huge. I hired two hundred people on the values of trust of management, trust of the culture, and trust in the strategy of the company to walk the talk. It was a much bigger company when I left, and it isn't always easy to hold on to your values when the company is so big, but sticking with our values actually made it prosper.

When I took the position of CEO at Northeast Delta Dental, I wanted to instill the same values there. Northeast Delta Dental had been around for a while. It was small and unknown, just kind of plodding along. However, since we instilled some of these values in it, our growth has been excellent. I have used many of the same success tenets here as I did in Massachusetts. Nowadays, because only 3.2 million people live in Maine, New Hampshire, and Vermont and so many of those people already have Delta Dental coverage, our growth has slowed somewhat. The next step is to start thinking about whether we need to be outside northern New England and offer other lines of coverage.

Even though I have had this sort of success running a values-driven organization, it can still feel difficult to maintain our values and succeed. Obviously, we have to make money. For instance, a few years ago, we put in a brand-new computer system that cost several million dollars. We had to do that to be competitive, but we tried to focus on sufficiency rather than greed. That's where I think Wall Street comes into play negatively for companies that have to deal with stockholders. It is much tougher for them to maintain values because they have a hard bottom line. In the final analysis, their sole goal is to make more money for the stockholders, whereas our objective is making enough to remain competitive while also giving back to the community.

Our model is successful because it is not about greed; it is about everybody taking a little bit of a hit and winding up generally happy. We really have to protect this model. Looking around, we see that most organizations have given into financial pressure. For instance, Blue Cross organizations used to be not for profit—they were run like we are—but many of them have been bought out by for-profit companies and their stockholders. After consolidation many decisions that in the past were made locally are now made elsewhere. This is true of New Hampshire Blue Cross that was bought out by Anthem of WellPoint, and it's been to the detriment of the citizens of New Hampshire ever since because the company doesn't invest as much in the community. Decisions aren't made locally; they're made in either Indiana or Connecticut. If you're running a local Blue Cross, Anthem will give you a budget, and if you use up that budget, you're done.

In theory, being bought out by a larger national company reduces the cost to the end user. This may be true in the short term, but it's not true in the long term. For one year administrative costs might be lower and the employers might get a lower price because of economy of scale, but in the long run will the employees be healthier? Will the service be as good if it is done by offshore service reps or a call center in Colorado or India? The feedback I've gotten is that the citizens of New Hampshire aren't as well off now. Thinking only about cost can be a disaster in the long run.

Our bottom line is values rather than finances. Northeast Delta Dental can still write a check for $10,000 for a community fund-raiser, and that's the end of it because the buck stops here. We are still able to meet the needs and challenges of the people in our community. If an employer comes to us and the company isn't doing well, I have the authority to help that company. For instance, Easter Seals is one of our customers, and one year it had a tough time because of flooding in Manchester. I was able to present the organization with a better price for that year. I know we will keep Easter Seals as a loyal customer for years to come.

If we were bought out by Delta Dental of California (which is a billion-dollar independent Delta plan and so can't buy us out, but let's say somehow it could), Concord Hospital, one of our biggest clients, might get a lower administrative rate, but Delta of California isn't going to give more than $50,000 in aid that we gave Concord Hospital during its fund-raising campaign for hospital expenses and a cancer center. If you sell out to a larger company, you might be able to cover your expenses today, but in the long run, you could lose your company and your values, and you could be working to the detriment of your community.

What We Learned

In this chapter our entrepreneurs shared stories that pointed to the core values that helped them learn to trust themselves. In order to go against industry norms and beat the odds, we have to learn to ground ourselves. Some of the cornerstones for getting the help we need to deal with the tough stuff are

- *Understand and be able to articulate your core values.* Listing your core values and keeping that list nearby can help you to trust yourself. As Carol points out, in order to trust yourself, you have to know yourself, and one of the ways to do this is to keep a journal or have a person you can talk to about who you are and what you value most in your life.

- *Turn toward your original mission to get grounded again.* Mission statements help to steer the boat when we are getting pulled in a lot of different directions. If someone offers a suggestion and you are not sure whether to take it, you might ask yourself if it meets your mission statement. Would you be adhering to or abandoning your mission by taking this suggestion?

- *Remember why you are in this business in the first place.* Usually we feel excitement when we are starting on a new venture. This excitement can serve to drive us forward in the beginning, but sometimes we lose sight of it as the business grows and we are dealing with various pressures. It can help to remember back to when the business first started and the excitement you felt about bringing your product or service into the world.

- *Believe in your product.* As Margot says, sometimes it is easier to believe in your product than it is to believe in yourself. If you remember the value of the product or service you are selling, you might feel more energy in terms of advocating it to the world and taking the necessary risks to beat the odds.

- *To paraphrase Mahatma Gandhi, hold on to the vision of the change you want to see in the world.* Don't forget that you aren't just making money. As Tom says, thinking only about cost can be a disaster in the long run. Remember that you are also doing something courageous: you are using your values-driven business to effect change in the world. If you need a reason to trust yourself, that could be it!

Throughout this book we tell our stories and offer tips to help get through the difficult times, the tough stuff. But we first turn to these core values to remind ourselves what is important.

Hire People in Your Company Who Know More Than You Do

Lisa tells the story of hiring her first general manager, who was the most highly paid employee at her company. She was terrified, but she knew her growing company needed a much higher level of baking and research and development skills than any of the current staff possessed. When he came on board, one of the first decisions he made saved the company an amount equal to more than his yearly salary and benefits. Over time she was relieved to see that he took over more and more of the operations part of the company, allowing her to focus on other areas.

4

Remembering to trust yourself

We love to hear stories from entrepreneurs who went against the grain. It's great to learn about the hero's journey, replete with overcoming all the odds. Rather than listening to conventional wisdom, these entrepreneurs trusted their instincts and believed their vision of what was possible. They found an innovative niche, explored fresh ways of connecting with their customers, and figured out how to stay ahead of the curve. During those early times of idealism and excitement, most entrepreneurs did everything themselves. They made the sales calls, developed the products, provided the services, wrote the checks, answered the phone, and swept the floor. This is an important part of the life cycle of a business. But if we remain in this mode, our companies will be only as strong as a single leader.

If we want our businesses to become sustainable enough to grow and create livable work for all stakeholders, then at some point the way we operate needs to shift. As this shift happens, we become more knowledgeable about our industries and begin to make use of conventional wisdom. At this point, we need to ask for help, know when to delegate, and know when to hire people who know more than we do. As we grow bigger, it can be difficult to keep track of our intuitive values and that gut feeling that started us off on the entrepreneurial road to begin with. We may start not to trust ourselves as much anymore.

In this chapter Lisa and Margot share stories about hiring "experts"—hires that led them to question their own knowledge of their companies. Joe tells us about a time he gave himself (and his work) away, a little at a time, and ended up not sticking with one of his own core values. Tom shares a story of questioning his own integrity in favor of looking good for his board. He illustrates how one small choice of straying from your standards can start a ripple effect. Marie talks about how sometimes there may be no way to stick to your mission, and the best choice left is compromise. When that happens you can reinvent yourself, start another project, and try to keep your original values intact.

These stories are about how we can stop trusting ourselves, a little at a time, until we don't know how we got to where we are and we have to find our way back. Sometimes we need to trust experts and sometimes we need to trust our own instincts. The trick is finding a balance.

Asking for Help Without Giving Yourself Away

■ **LISA**

After many years at Vermont Bread Company, I finally delegated the role of sales manager to someone highly recommended by my former business partner. This person was bright, articulate, and confident. He had previous marketing experience, which I hoped would make up for my complete lack of knowledge in this area. At the end of the first year his results were disappointing. He kept telling us he couldn't close sales because we needed to offer better promotional programs with deeper discounts, create new products and product line extensions, and restructure our pricing to give higher margins to our customers.

During the second year he told me repeatedly that the marketplace was completely different than when I was overseeing sales. "It's just not as easy as it was back then," he would tell me when a new customer didn't sign up. I believed him because I figured he knew more than I did. I started to worry about the future of our company because growth seemed to have slowed so much. Within the next few months, as sales continued to stagnate, he decided our company was not able to give him the opportunities he was looking for, and he resigned. Until I could find a replacement, I had to step back into the sales role, and I was dreading it.

After a few weeks on the road, I found that what he had told me was not actually true. It was then that I realized how easily I had let his knowledge and experience trump mine. When I called on new potential customers, told my story, served them Vermont Bread toast, and presented our programs, I was able to close sales as I always had. And I realized I had given my knowledge away for what I thought was an expert's experience.

When you stop trusting yourself, it is often connected to self-doubt. We think we are not capable, so we trust an "expert" more than we trust ourselves and decide someone else knows better than we do how to make decisions about our companies. We need to find a balance between asking for help and understanding that what we know is enough. While we are learning the ropes, we will inevitably make a mess. We have to know when it is past time for us to stop making a mess and be able to say, "This is not working." One way to know when something is not working is to take a hard look at the results. The sales manager I hired had a long resume and a reputation of being very good. He told me a lot of stories about what he was doing, and I saw him move around a lot, but the results were poorer than what I had seen when I was doing his job.

A lot of movement and talking does not always mean results. Sometimes you might see someone make weird, circuitous movements and hear very little from her, yet the results tell the true story of her success. For instance, a full-loaf packaging machine in the bakery slices the bread, bags it, and puts a closure on it. The guy who runs it is nicknamed Earl. He has been running it for years, and when brand-new employees come in and see him, they think he's not doing much of anything. Earl is a big guy, and he stands in one place appearing relaxed and unproductive. The truth is, he is very skilled at his job—he has the working of that machine down to a science. If he is there, that machine runs perfectly. If you put someone else on that machine, that person runs around like crazy and appears to be working really hard, but when you look at the machine, you see it is not running smoothly.

Results should speak the loudest. A well-respected expert in your company might tell you, "Your product is flawed, your company is flawed, and I am going to do such and such to help you make it right." But when you actually look at the results, you might see that production or sales numbers have actually gone down. Of course, in order to grow your company, you have to ask for help, but asking for help does not have to mean giving yourself away or not trusting yourself.

For over thirteen years I ran Vermont Bread Company with a business partner. We never saw each other outside of work, but every day we came into our company and worked together to run it. When we became a grown-up company with a factory and systems and policies, my partner did not want anything to do with it. He liked the entrepreneurial, seat-of-the-pants, creative decision making of a start-up. So he left the company and built a beautiful house outside Portland, Maine. But he forgot two very important facts: he is a pilot and I am a very convincing salesperson. I kept talking him into flying back to Vermont to help me. He decided he had picked the wrong Portland and moved to Portland, Oregon—you cannot easily fly a Cessna from Oregon to Vermont.

When I finally accepted that he was really gone, I floundered for a while and then made two key decisions: first, to hire people who knew way more that I did and, second, to create an active advisory board (see the "Practical Wisdom" section at the end of this chapter). I do a lot of one-on-one consulting at events like Social Venture Institute, and my key advice is always this: Put together an advisory board. Look around at your networks and try to pick people who really know their stuff. For my advisory board, I needed people who were strong enough to stand up to me because I can be a steamroller. I got a banker, a baker, some owners of bigger businesses, an attorney, and a marketing person. Over the years, whenever I had outgrown a particular board, I would take the members out to a nice dinner and politely fire them. Then I would find people with experience running larger companies who could help us get to the next level.

Having an advisory board gives you a place where you can lift up your head and look to the future. I am a real fan of advisory boards—for businesses and for life in general. (We are actually playing with a model in Vermont called the Chess Club to provide an advisory board for your life and career.) Creating a board gives you a group of people who have made a commitment to understanding your issues and your history. I always retain complete veto power over all my board's decisions; that way, I always have at least one place in my professional life where I can ask for help and yet never have to give myself away.

The Professionals Versus the Spirit in the Box

■ MARGOT

The bigger a company becomes, the harder it is for an entrepreneur to stick to her vision and remember to trust herself. When a company reaches a certain size, you have to delegate tasks, and you can't control everything. You often lose track of what is going on in different areas of your company. When I started Birkenstock, I vowed to run it like a company I would want to work in myself. I had worked as a dress designer in Canada, and that was the only time in my life I was an employee and had my place in the hierarchy. I worked on the designs, made the patterns, oversaw the sample makers, and fitted the dresses on the models. Because the company was big, I never found out how the whole business fit together, where the profits came from, or how the salesmen sold the goods. I loved the dressmaking work, but because I was not connected to the enterprise, I felt isolated and dissatisfied. I decided if I ever ran a company, my employees would never feel that way.

This was a very good intention, but this sort of ideal is hard to stick with as the company gets bigger. When Birkenstock was small, it was easy. I didn't have to face the challenge of losing track of the vision or forgetting to trust myself. I had close relationships with my staff, my supplier, and my retailers in the field. My staff consisted of two people: a bookkeeper/secretary and a stockboy. They knew everything that was going on, and I consulted them whenever I had a question. I told them about the goals we wanted to achieve, and then I would ask, "How do you think we should do that? Do you have any ideas?" In this way, they became part of the business. We all worked together, and it was fun.

We called the company Birkenstock Footprint Sandals, Inc., but we didn't own the brand; it was the Birkenstock family name, and I worked closely with Mr. Birkenstock. Only five years before I discovered his shoes, he'd been baking the first footbed in his mother's oven. We grew our companies together. When I first went to Germany to visit him, he had a staff of about sixty employees, including manufacturing and selling. Again, because his business was small, I became familiar with its whole process and with the German staff. Mr. Birkenstock frequently came to the United States as well. When we traveled together, so he could understand the American market, he sometimes brought his family along. So I knew his three sons from the time they were babies. On our travels we formed very close relationships with all of our retailers. It was important to have those connections because the retailers were carrying our mission into their communities and needed all the information about the product they could get. We held annual conventions for them, and Mr. Birkenstock often attended those. The middle years were the best for me: I retained the vision of running an "ideal" company, and everyone was connected to all aspects of the process. It was a very personal business, and I enjoyed it very much.

But as we grew, I started to doubt myself more. I began to ask, "Am I really cut out to run this place?" Though this question weighed on my mind, I never mentioned it to anybody because *grow bigger we must.* That is always the mantra of business. Frequently, that is also why trouble starts: during growth a lot of entrepreneurs start losing track of their visions. They begin to give themselves away rather than trusting in their missions. For instance, I had always tried to promote our own people from within so that I knew what I was getting. But as the company grew, we needed advanced skills in different areas, and I decided to hire "professionals." The first one was a sales manager who was well known in the industry. When he joined us, he hired his sales team. They didn't understand that

Birkenstock was more than meeting quotas, earning commissions, and manipulating retailers into buying more than they needed. Before I knew it, I had a department of people more focused on making money than on building relationships with our customers. I had, in a sense, given my vision away.

To me it was clear: in order for a business to be sustainable in the long term, the relationships have to matter more than the high sales numbers. When I did the selling myself, I never tried to oversell. I never pushed people into buying more. I took into consideration that they would have to pay for the merchandise. I wanted to be sure we could count on the money coming in. My way of thinking was odd to most salesmen, and this sales team was no different. Because I knew about the tendency for salesmen to focus on high numbers, for years our sales folks were on straight salary. That didn't fly with this "professional sales force," so, I caved in, and we worked out a quarterly bonus system based on volume. The bonuses would be paid out, but four months later a retailer might still return the shoes. What then? At that point I felt I was standing still and trains were rushing by in both directions. I was getting dizzy. I had given my vision away. Finally, I woke up and said, "This is not working." I had to fire a number of the salespeople, but luckily, I didn't have to fire all of them—some had begun to understand.

As a company grows bigger, it can be important for the growing staff to understand the spirit in which you started the business. But sometimes it can be difficult to translate this spirit into words. That's where our Birki Boy came in. Years ago, at an international distributor meeting that Birkenstock held in Germany, the Dutch distributor spoke about the almost mysterious way Birkenstock sandals had spread out into the world. He attributed the footwear's success to an invisible spirit inside each box. Its magic unfolded once the box was opened. As with all fairy tales, you had to believe in it before it could manifest itself. I wanted to make the intangible tangible—I wanted to express to my staff the spirit in which I started Birkenstock. So I had a very talented employee create a hand puppet: the Birki Boy. He was the "spirit made visible." We used this character at retailer meetings with great success. He helped us tell the story. After the fallout from hiring and then firing the sales force had died down, I realized it was time to get the Birki Boy out of his hiding place again. At the next sales meeting, he told our crew that they'd better start believing in him because without him, Birkenstock would not be where it is today.

Sometimes you think you can hold on to your mission by hiring people who hold the same values as you do. But just because someone talks about values doesn't mean that person will necessarily be able to act with integrity. For example, when I hired the consultant for our succession plan, I believed I was hiring someone sensitive, capable, and socially responsible. This man worked with us for a while and got to know Birkenstock, and then he suggested we do some team building and bonding via a weekend of togetherness at a nearby Zen center. The program entailed a variety of exercises, including falling trustingly into the arms of others. One young salesman was very afraid of the trust exercises, but we finally got him to fall backward into our outstretched arms. It was a tremendous achievement for him.

Two days later, the consultant and our sales manager fired the young man. Even before the team-building weekend began, they had known they were going to let him go. Together, they had decided they should run the show, they knew what was best, and I should take a step back and let them handle matters. I did not feel good about that at all: this young salesman had trusted in a way that was very scary to him, and now he was being fired. You can't play with people's emotions like that.

In turn, I wound up firing both the consultant and the sales manager.

In the end, I followed my own conviction, but often you can't know what will happen from the beginning. It is difficult to identify which people will take the power you offer and abuse it. You just have to deal with the results as best you can. I did not give up on consultants: I continued to hire them. Their outsider perspective was very important to me, and they remained a valuable resource for our success. I just had to know how to use their advice—what to embrace and what to disregard. A few years later I met the succession consultant again. We were on a program together, he as a speaker and I as a panel member. We talked, and he acknowledged his mistake. He said he totally understood my reaction.

What I learned from these adventures is that you can't always be right. Sometimes your trust in others is misplaced, and situations don't turn out so well. I have been called too trusting at times, but I would rather be disappointed once in a while than to live as a suspicious and paranoid character every day. After all, when I did trust myself again, I was always able to remedy the situation.

Giving Yourself Away One Step at a Time

■ JOE, CREATIVE MACHINES

Sometimes I don't even realize I'm not trusting myself and following my value system, but I wind up accepting a job because I think it is going to be good for the community. Later I realize I've made a number of concessions, I haven't kept my values or my boundaries, and I'm in over my head. The result is like throwing one stone into a pond and watching a bad ripple effect.

It is against my principles to work for less money than something is worth, yet last year I gave myself away by not following that value closely enough. I didn't follow it closely enough because it conflicted with another value: I like to do work that is going to make the world a better place. At Creative Machines, we sometimes do public art projects for the community, and I won a public art commission for Ochoa Park in Tucson, just north of the South Tucson border. The park is by a ravine, and a school nearby is being closed because it's in bad shape. A lot of "bad" people apparently get together in the park and shoot out the three street lights so they can deal drugs. Kids are afraid to play in the park, and drug dealers are always popping up out of the ravine, and there's a lot of shooting everything up. They shoot holes in the boxes that run the sprinklers and other objects at the park. So, the Arts Council had a contest for a public art project to try to keep kids in the park and make it a more interesting place to play and hang out. Only $10,000 was available for it, and since that really isn't enough to create public art, I didn't even enter—yet I still won.

This is what happened. I have a friend at the Arts Council, and she called me one day and said, "I sort of added your name to the list because you do a lot of things that might help them. You are an inventor and a creator, you come up with economical and unusual solutions, and maybe you could figure out how to give them good lighting. The city really didn't give them enough good street lamps." And I said, "Oh, geez, thanks!" but I didn't take my name off the list. That was my first concession. For the Arts Council presentation, I brought a video of something we created in our shop that I call public drums, which is a rugged structure secured on a metal base. You can tap anywhere on them to make music. At the presentation, I said, "If people have a really good time and are drawn to be there, maybe they'll come to respect it." But I also said, "You guys don't need public art. You need police protection." All too often, public art is asked to do the job that city planners and architects bungled while the real problem falls through the cracks. Public art is expected to revitalize an area or, as in this case, to stop crime. I said, "The only way we can make something like this is to get more money for it. The city would have to agree to run power to the location and give me a concrete pad to set the structure on. There would need to be another source of money, so I don't expect that you would want me to do this." And then I left.

Well, I got a call the following week that the committee really liked what I had said, and they selected me. After a month, the city couldn't commit to any more funds because of the bad economy. I told the Arts Council people, "I didn't promise anything unless I can have a concrete block and electricity going into it." The Arts Council people said, "Tucson Electric Power has a few leftover solar panels and batteries from another public art project. They'll give you those for your power source." When I told them I would have to put the solar panel up on a ten-foot pole so nobody would shoot it, they replied, "We'll see if we can get it donated." I said, "Maybe there'll be some more money." And they said, "No, there won't be."

If there had been more money in the budget, I could have simply run electricity to the location and would have been able to do a better design. I spent an inordinate amount of time trying to figure out how to protect a solar panel and battery. They're pretty vulnerable objects. I thought about bailing out, but I was in far enough that it would have looked bad. That's how a lot of difficult situations happen: you keep taking baby steps. One thought that kept me going was that I shouldn't run from tough challenges if I want to make money. If Tucson has a dangerous park situation that I can solve, chances are a hundred cities across the country have similar problems. If I could make something that worked in this park and didn't cost a fortune, perhaps I could turn it into a product and sell it nationally.

Finally things started looking up. A retiring Parks and Recreation employee was very interested in the project and was able to get the city to donate the labor to dig a trench from a nearby junction box. The poor economy let me hire an electrical contractor to run power in the trench for a very good price. I came up with a design that I liked. The drums are about the size of conga drums. Their surface is touch sensitive and glows at night. They are made of bulletproof polycarbonate (similar to drive-through windows at fast-food restaurants in really bad neighborhoods where you have to put your money into the slot). My employee Eric was my destructive tester because he was a juvenile delinquent when he was little. He banged on the drums with a pickax and used his lighter to try to burn through them. The project has proven successful with the public. Local residents love it, no one has hurt it, and I enjoy visiting so that I can watch people play with it. I'm working with playground equipment reps to try to market something like it nationally.

This story will probably have a successful ending, but I still wonder if I did the right thing because I came close to violating a basic principle. Essentially, I was doing $50,000 worth of work for a $10,000 grant. The problem with this form of charity is that other artists who are given $10,000 grants will be expected to do $50,000 worth of work. When asked to do charity, we sometimes forget that work (or the sale of products) is never performed in a vacuum; it is always done within an existing economic system upon which some people depend. I think the lesson I've taken away from this is to keep looking toward my basic principles and continue to ask myself at every turn, "Am I following my values?" We tend to think that because we are doing charity and working for a good cause, we should do it for less money than it's worth. But there is a narrow segment within which charity prevents good economic exchange. It can make it hard to sell something for a fair price. Part of the work we do as values-driven businesspeople is to make a sustainable living so that we can keep on giving.

The Moment of Truth

■ **TOM, NORTHEAST DELTA DENTAL**

It can be difficult to continue to trust in your values while you are trying to succeed, particularly on a personal level. For instance, at Northeast Delta Dental we have a very sophisticated CEO review process evaluation and succession plan called a 360. Everybody participates in it. A few years ago the board members said they would like to see the 360 reviews that the people who work with me had written. I really want the reviews because they have been very meaningful to me in terms of growth, but sometimes they are hard hitting, and it can be nerve-wracking to think of your boss reading people's comments out of context. I've had moments when I've sat in my office and seriously thought about how I can make the reviews look better than they are. I have asked myself questions like, "Do I really want to show them this?" "Can I sanitize this?"

That's the truth—I really have asked those questions. Those aren't my best moments and ultimately I know that I have to show everything to the board. I have to adhere to my value of honesty and transparency first, and then I need to handle the fallout, whatever that might be. It's the right answer. But I'm sure everybody goes through that kind of struggle.

At these times, it is usually good to remember that all the different problems in corporate America probably start with something that seems easy, like fooling with a review report, something relatively gray and small. And then that dishonesty grows to the point where you are doing something illicit, something that takes you down the path of duplicity and corruption. I can see how that could happen. But if you keep trusting in your core values to see you through, you almost always make the right choice.

When Societal Pressures Impinge on the Mission

■ **MARIE, MS. FOUNDATION AND THE WHITE HOUSE PROJECT**

Sometimes you have a great mission—it is timely and innovative and you know the world needs it—yet societal pressures are too much for your funding sources, and you find yourself having to move away from your vision. This happened with our Ms. Foundation for Women program. Our mission was to raise the expectations of girls in the United States. One way we did this was to create Take Our Daughters to Work Day. But the minute the last girl walked out of the workplace on the first Take Our Daughters to Work Day, the cry went up: "What about the boys?" While many fathers were thrilled about the program, some men were outraged, and others were sincerely concerned.

One congresswoman said we needed a Take Our Sons to Work Day like we needed a White History Month. Nonetheless, throughout the life of the program, we bent over backward to see how we could help resolve the conflict. We convened male leaders who contacted us, and we explained the event's mission. We offered to take their sons to work in places where men were in the minority, like childcare centers. They flatly refused this suggestion, saying it would punish their sons. Nothing would do but that we take their boys to work just like we were doing with the girls. We were a small women's organization. It wasn't that we didn't want to help boys—we had sons and knew that not all boys were doing well—but the girls were all we could manage. We did use Take Our Daughters to Work to talk about problems boys were having, too, including issues of class and race and how difficult it is to awaken to the issues of the minority when you are in the majority. Still, the men didn't support the program. They pressed lawsuits, picketed our building, and threatened us with violence.

We remained committed to our mission until the culture finally got the upper hand. Women had begun to feel disloyal to their sons and joined participating workplaces in insisting that they add boys. Some companies called it Take Our Children to Work Day but kept focusing the day on girls. Others just started adding boys. The broth of the day got thinner and thinner. The day had never received much financial support, regardless of its enormous adoption across the country and even beyond. It was designed as a stand-alone program. Companies could implement it without acknowledging the Ms. Foundation or supporting it financially. That made us very dependent on certain funding sources. Finally, the company that had given us the most money and hung in with us the longest called to say the internal criticism was too difficult to withstand. We had to include boys and rename the program in order for them to give us any more support.

I looked for other money for girls only, but there was none to be had. We took the issue to the board members, who wisely told us to resist doing the Take Our Children day, but consider Take Our Daughters and Sons to Work. Then we called in folks to help us design activities for girls *and* boys. We built on research by work-life organizations showing that our daughters and sons want a family-friendly work world that allows them to be involved in all areas of their lives—family, work, and community—without penalty. We partnered with these organizations and let the companies know about the new name and activities. By then, almost all of them were including boys in some way and were relieved when the program was renamed Take Our Daughters and Sons to Work Day.

When we added the boys, many women knew that this would once again dilute the attention to girls' aspirations, and they were rightfully angry. They couldn't get us money to run the original program, but that didn't stop them from letting us know what we already felt: we had failed our nation's daughters. We gave ourselves away and strayed from our original mission.

The original conflict had propelled the overwhelming press and success that Take Our Daughters to Work Day garnered every year. Once it became Take Our Daughters and Sons to Work, the controversy was over, and the press wasn't interested. The controversy had actually helped generate conversations about women and men, work and family, and the changing roles of our sons and daughters. After the name change, the issue lacked spark. Girls fell off the front pages, literally.

The day for daughters and sons still exists, under the stewardship of a terrific couple who worked with our foundation for years. Wherever I go to speak about the importance of women's leadership, grown women come up to me and say they learned about their careers by going to work with their parents or a friend's parent. At the White House Project, we now sponsor Take Our Daughters to the Polls to stress the importance of putting women in leadership roles. We still have to deal with the societal pressure to support boys and not make waves. When this sort of pressure starts to impinge on funding sources, it can be almost impossible for the original mission to survive, and you might find yourself giving yourself away, but hopefully you can regenerate your ideas in another arena that will make a difference in the world.

What We Learned

It helps to know whether to continue to trust the experts or trust your own gut. Here is some advice that might be helpful:

- *Set a reasonable time limit to evaluate.* When we are used to doing everything ourselves, we can find it difficult to delegate and step aside so the work can be done differently. Don't expect results too quickly, but do find a reasonable timeline to begin to see the outcomes that your business needs.

- *Measure the results.* Even if the work is not being done in the way you would do it, you can ask yourself some questions in order to find out if the new way is effective. Are sales better? Is the gross margin expanding? Has the environmental impact been reduced? Is morale high on the team? Has quality been enhanced? Are customers happy? Has profit increased? Whatever your expectation was for the new way of doing things, find a way to measure it and use the result to inform your decisions.

- *Understand that sometimes it isn't your fault.* Marie and the Ms. Foundation couldn't have done anything differently in terms of Take Our Daughters to Work. If they had insisted on excluding boys, they would have lost all their funding and the project would have been disbanded. Sometimes the best you can do is to compromise (at least girls are still going to work, even though boys are also going), and that is okay. If it's not your fault, don't beat yourself up. Marie's organization is now sponsoring Take

Our Daughters to the Polls, which fits her original mission of supporting and empowering girls.

- *Ask your advisory board.* When you feel unsure, this is a good time to get the support and clarity that your advisory board can provide. If you have chosen well, the members can collectively help you find the perspective you need.

These steps can provide the balance between trusting ourselves and getting the help our company needs to succeed.

■ PRACTICAL TIP

Spend Time Offering Appreciation

Positive energy can be infectious. Here are some ways to spread it:

- Handwrite thank-you notes to employees, vendors, or customers.

- Verbally offer praise.

- Use the Recognition Circle: tell employees something wonderful that other employees or managers have told you about them.

■ PRACTICAL TIP

Tackle Another Business Owner Who Has "Been There" and Confess

This tip was offered by Tami Simon of Sounds True Recording as one of the ten best ways to get the most out of a Social Venture Network gathering. The person you confess to does not need to be in a similar industry, the same geographic region, or an equal-size organization, as long as he is self-reflective, tells the truth about his own experiences, and is willing to engage about the important issues you are struggling with.

Create an Advisory Board

What has helped during the tough times? Honestly, getting help! An advisory board can be a lifeline. This is a place to talk about your business, share your challenges, discuss your numbers, seek out new revenue streams, talk through problems with key employees, and figure out the next steps. It's a place to lift your head up, away from those feet that are stomping out the daily fires.

Definition and Role of an Advisory Board

There are no hard-and-fast rules about advisory boards, but some of the basics are

- Advisory board members are consultants to the CEO and are selected by the CEO.
- Board members represent a variety of functional expertise and experiences.
- An advisory board provides someone to talk to—leading a values-based business *is* lonely.
- The board has no fiduciary responsibility.
- The board can be as large or small a group as you want it to be.
- The board can be formal or informal.
- The goal of an advisory board is to help the CEO do a better job and be a better leader in creating a sustainable, healthy company.

Ten Tips for Creating Your Advisory Board

Following are some tips that will help you create an advisory board.

1. *Search out people who know more than you do.* Most entrepreneurs are either experts in a functional area or generalists (which is a fancy way of saying they aren't experts at anything). It is important to know what you don't know and then surround yourself with people who know more than you do in areas critical for achieving success in all your bottom lines.
2. *Find people who can stand up to you.* People who work for you are inclined to agree with you. Even members of your board of directors are often likely to be friends who know you well. For an advisory board to be effective, you need honest feedback, so it is important to get people who are willing to say, "That's an interesting idea, but have you thought of this?"
3. *Don't be afraid to ask!* The inclination is to ask only people you know well to be on your advisory board. But the key is to identify the areas where you need the most support and find people who are best able to give that support to you. You will probably be surprised by how many people are willing to help. (They can learn a ton, too, from the other smart people around the table.)
4. *Be prepared to have regular meetings, with one or two e-mail updates between meetings.* It helps to have a more formal meeting structure that reinforces the seriousness of the board. Prepare as you would for a regular board of directors meeting. At least a week in advance of the advisory board meeting, send the board members an agenda, a president's report identifying current issues, and recent financial statements. If you do this, the board will take the work more seriously, and you will get better and more meaningful feedback.

5. *Feed them (and water them and caffeinate them).* These people are spending their precious free time with you focusing on your business, so treat them well—it shows respect for their role and their advice.

6. *Pay them.* Paying your advisory board members reinforces the value of the advice you are asking for and shows that their effort and input are important. The payment also helps you to take the meeting preparation more seriously. It doesn't have to be a lot of money, but your focus and the board's focus is improved if you show you are serious by paying for the members' time. Some people pay $100 or $250 or $500 per meeting. Do what fits with the size of your business and the status of your cash flow.

7. *Have part of the meeting at your company, but then leave.* The board needs to stay connected to your business— your physical plant, your employees, your signage, and so on. But only part of your meeting time should be spent at the company because (you know it's true) you will be interrupted. Get an off-site meeting room where you can shut the door. Often you can get one inexpensively at a restaurant, your bank, or your lawyer's office.

8. *Set aside your ego and tell the truth.* Meetings are a good time to really listen to the smart people you have assembled. Don't be defensive; these folks are here to help you. They are people with shoulders to cry on, people to complain to, and people from whom you can get help to become a better CEO and get the best advice to grow your company to the next level. Don't be afraid to try out new ideas with them. It's better to practice with them than to stumble in front of your banker or a major customer.

9. *Spend time assessing what is working with the board and what is not.* After each meeting, conduct a critical review: Did you get good feedback on the issues raised? Did everyone participate? Did the format work? What could you have done better to make the time more productive? How could you make the next meeting more effective?

10. *Don't be afraid to change your board as your needs change.* Times change, your business changes, and you change. What was once an appropriate composition of the board may not be appropriate now. Assess whether you need to replace various members or the board as a whole. Present a nice speech, give a long toast, acknowledge all that you have accomplished together—and then bring in the next board.

Sample Agenda

What has worked in other companies is to keep meetings loose but structured; bring in key staff members to do presentations—it gives them practice and lets the board assess the team; leave enough time to have significant discussions; and stick to the timelines. Here's a sample agenda:

Advisory Board Meeting, September xx, 20xx

3:00 - 3:30	Tour plant to see new production line (plant manager)
3:30 - 4:00	Review new marketing materials (vice president of marketing)
4:00 - 4:30	Go over the numbers (controller)
4:30 - 5:00	Check in on issues raised at last meeting, and frame the "big questions" from today's meeting (CEO)
5:00 - 5:30	Move to private dining room at local inn
5:30 - 8:00	Dinner and discussion

Attached to this agenda are the following:

- Quarterly financials
- Key production numbers and other "pulse points" measured by the company
- Memo (brain dump) from CEO, including updates on five issues, problems, projects, or opportunities with questions and concerns flagged

Build Your Advisory Board

Take five minutes to think about who might be a good fit for your new advisory board. What skills could complement yours to take your organization to the next level? Whom do you admire who can push you to think more deeply about

- Growing your revenue?
- Marketing differently, a new perspective?
- Finding new opportunities, another revenue stream?
- Developing a more sustainable organization?
- Owning your numbers and understanding them (*all* of them)?
- Creating a new rhythm within your organization to facilitate better communication?
- Reducing your carbon or water use footprint even more?
- Managing people better?
- Taking better care of yourself?
- Creating more value in your company?

Think of people who

- Run a company that is bigger than yours
- Run a similar or smaller organization that does some things better than you do

- Have a specific area of expertise (for example, accounting, legal, social responsibility, marketing, human resources)
- Have recently retired within your industry

Mix it up! Get a diverse group around your table. Think about various age groups, lengths of time in business, types of organizations, genders, races, political points of view, and so on.

Now list the names of five people and make a commitment to invite each one to become a member of your advisory board.

1. _____

2. _____

3. _____

4. _____

5. _____

I will contact all five by _____ , 20_____ .

Signature _____

Good luck with your new board!

Wrestling with Goliath

We use "Goliath" as shorthand for the things we face in business that seem overwhelming and impossible. We may feel like no matter what size our companies become, someone or something is always bigger. Perhaps a key employee who provides a knowledge base you don't have threatens to quit or a big customer says she'll drop your services unless you drop your price (even when you have grown your business to accommodate her company and it represents 30 percent of your volume). This is the chapter about those big things that wake you up in the middle of the night. You lie in bed worried about your family and how to provide for them, the eighty or so other families who count on your company for their livable wages and health insurance coverage, the community programs that depend on your sponsorship, and whether your business can keep going for the long term or even until next week.

You are not the only one who has been there. Lisa starts us out with a story about her largest distributor getting into financial trouble that spilled over into her business and put the entire company at risk. Margot remembers how her largest customer dropped her entire line after she had ramped up to meet the projected orders for the next year. Joe tells us how a previous client called him and claimed he'd stolen an idea and had no right to use it. In times like these, adrenaline courses through your body. You feel like you've been punched in the stomach, and you fear that everything you have built is a house of cards that can come tumbling down. These times feel like the toughest of the tough stuff. At the end of this chapter, we distill a few reminders that have helped us when we faced our own Goliaths.

The Multilegged Stool Rule, or Don't Put All Your Eggs in That Solid-Looking Basket

■ **LISA**

My Goliath story is about dealing with a great distributor in the Boston area when Vermont Bread Company was in its early years. This distributor grew at 50 percent per year, did all of our billing, and made all of the calls to store buyers, and his sales volume represented over half the total sales by our company. We were quite fat and happy—until one day we weren't. After a decade of rapidly growing his business (and ours), our distributor got involved with a shady crowd and was persuaded to move his assets into a shell public company. That was the last anyone saw of his assets. He started kiting checks and whistling and dancing on the collection calls from us. When the dust settled he owed us $195,000.

At the time, we were not a large company, and we had only a $50,000 line of credit. We were sweating. Our stores started calling and screaming about poor service and out-of-stock products. One chain refused to sell our bread until we could resolve our issues. There was no other independent distributor in this market, so making a switch wasn't an option. And starting our own distribution company was beyond our limited resources.

Even though we could have come up with several ideas we would have liked to do to that distributor, we had to focus on finding solutions. How in the world would we keep going, pay our bills, and meet payroll this week? We searched our network and found a great lawyer who could help us negotiate with the new owners (the original guy and his new partners) of the distribution company. We agreed to continue to supply them if they gave us a $75,000 down payment on what we were owed. Luckily, they did, so we had enough for payroll for a while. Then we needed to find sources of cash to help us through. My partners and I cut our pay. I did a reforecast. We used our personal credit cards to pay bills. Unfortunately, it just wasn't enough to plug the cash flow hole left by the distributor. We still needed to find a short-term cash answer.

Out of desperation, we did what most entrepreneurs never want to do: we swallowed our pride and admitted our mistakes. We acknowledged to ourselves that we never should have let this one customer become large enough to have the power to sink us. It was our failure for not balancing his sales with other revenues. Knowing that gave us the tools to get out of the mess in the long term. We called our bank—the one that had given us the $50,000 line of credit—and our suppliers, and we told them what had happened and said that we needed help. The bankers and suppliers responded well because we had never blindsided them. We had a history of telling them the bad news as well as the good news. We paid our bills when we could and called them with a plan when we needed them. We got extended terms in exchange for loyalty and regular updates. Our suppliers and bankers helped us get through, and we learned something valuable in the process: the importance of the multilegged stool. If a stool has just one or two legs, it will fall over. In business terms, you need to match your largest accounts with others of equal or larger size.

Remembering the multilegged stool rule really helps as your business grows bigger and larger accounts come your way. It might seem easier to just stay small and not deal with big Goliaths, but I sometimes feel frustrated when people try to convince me that small is beautiful. You can't really say no to a big account because then you are saying no to growth. If you say no, you stay very small. If you say yes, then your next job is to find another account that is equal in size to that one. This was a lesson that kept smacking me upside the head while I was at Vermont Bread Company: *Don't put all your eggs in that nice, solid-looking basket.*

This solid-looking basket rule kept returning for us. In a time of consolidation of customers and suppliers, most of us in food manufacturing were facing this problem again and again. In our case, when I sold Vermont Bread Company, we were scrambling to match our largest and best customer. This customer was only one-third of the way through build-out plans for the East Coast and still growing fast. It would have been so easy to be lulled into ignoring the multilegged stool rule. This company was easy to deal with, its leaders loved us, its corporate values were aligned with ours, it paid its bills early, it never took a credit, and it grew at over 50 percent per year. We worked so hard just to keep up with it, but we knew from experience we had to balance it out. One way to remedy this is to always have a multilegged stool that won't fall over if one leg is pulled out from under you.

We did survive the distributor disaster, and when a company comes through something like that, the memory becomes the story of a hero's victory—or, to quote a friend, "more fun in the telling than the doing." In the middle of it, we never felt like heroes. Embracing our values of transparency and honest communication in the midst of a significant financial crisis like that one can be really tough. You are not always sure you can survive. But Goliath is not as tall as he looks. You usually do survive to tell the tale. And the lessons you learn from it can be invaluable as you journey forth.

When Smaller Is Better

■ MARGOT

I was always a little afraid of large companies. I didn't think they would really know how to sell Birkenstocks because a customer needs education. Customers can't just pull Birkenstocks off the shelf like they can other shoes. People who have never worn Birkenstocks before might think the shoes don't fit and they're too odd. For this reason, I started out selling to individual retailers. I would tell them about the shoes so they could educate their customers. I liked working that way, but of course as the company got bigger, larger companies became interested in selling the product. It is difficult to say no to that kind of growth.

The first large company I dealt with was Nordstrom. Nordstrom is a prestigious account, especially for shoes. If your shoe brand is in *Nordstrom,* you feel you have arrived. The first Nordstrom account that came to us was a men's department in Portland, Oregon. I went to the store and trained the salespeople so they could educate customers about buying Birkenstocks. This department did very well for several years until the manager was promoted to a different position and the sales dwindled. In the meantime, other Nordstrom stores in other cities had bought our shoes, and we had trained their salespeople. But when customers saw them on the shelves, they didn't necessarily buy them. Because the salespeople were compensated in terms of how many shoes they sold each day, they didn't want to spend half an hour with a customer, educating the person about Birkenstocks and hoping for one sale. The excellent results in Portland were entirely due to the manager there, who understood the product and was a champion for it.

Even when a big company is a huge supporter of your product, that is still not enough sometimes. In another department store in Costa Mesa, the manager of the women's shoe department was enthusiastic about our product and had given us big orders at first. Then all of a sudden, we didn't hear from her anymore. I called the buyer and asked why she wasn't ordering our sandals. She said, "We are selling them very well. As a matter of fact, I'm out of them, and I'm sending customers who ask for them to a nearby retail store that carries Birkenstock because I can't buy any more from you. We buy sandals as a department category, and we are totally overstocked with other shoes. We have to sell all of those before we can buy more of yours."

When you sell to large companies, another problem you run into is competition. Larger companies have a tremendous amount of resources, and they might decide to copy your product, sell it at a lower price, and undermine your sales. A couple of years later, we sold to L.L.Bean. At first we sold to the big retail store in Maine. I visited the sales manager and explained the shoes to him so he would understand how to educate the customer. The store was huge. It was open twenty-four hours a day, and the manager of the shoe department was very good to us. He sold Birkenstocks at full price for two years. Then the mail-order department wanted to talk to us. Our salespeople went to Maine, and L.L.Bean put our shoes in the catalog for a number of years.

Business was wonderful until the company decided to put a similar, cheaper product in the same catalog a few pages after ours. We had no warning that L.L.Bean was going to do this. The price difference was enormous, and our sales numbers started dropping. We had expected a big catalog order but then had to scramble to redo our forecast. We were now asking ourselves, "How can we get the necessary cash to keep us afloat? To whom can we turn for additional credit?" We had budgeted for and anticipated sales that never materialized. We couldn't sue the company because we didn't have a copyright on the design of the shoe; we had only a copyright on the name "Birkenstock." The parent German company never thought of patenting the design. We did inquire about it, but by then it was too late—a company can't do a retroactive patent. Because of our name recognition, if L.L.Bean had used the word "Birkenstock" in the catalog, we would have been able to take some action.

This situation had an impact on everyone, including our supplier and our customer base. Our supplier, the Birkenstock company in Germany, was just as affected as we were, having built up manufacturing capacity and ordered supplies for the sales. Having to tell our contacts there that these sales would not materialize was embarrassing and humiliating. It helped that we had built a solid relationship with them over the years. We were able to cancel some orders and delay the shipment of others that had already been produced.

Our customers were also affected. They suffered the most from the price-cutting L.L.Bean introduced into the marketplace. Independent retailers made up our largest customer base. Somehow we had to come up with ways to help them. Other suppliers might have adversarial relationships with their retailers, just trying to get the most profit out of a deal, but I believed we would do well only when our resellers could also prosper. We decided to create special-edition products, styles, and colors just for them. We gave them complete marketing materials to go along with these products; then we sold them at promotional prices. These special products took a while to produce, and in the meantime we were running "lean and mean" at headquarters. Everybody pitched in. Our bankers were understanding. They were inquisitive about how we were going to replace the lost volume, but they trusted us to pull it off, and we did.

This story is about holding on to the value of quality over cost. Doing this can be very difficult when an entrepreneur is facing the Goliath of a competitive market. Quality and price are often at war in the marketplace. Well-meaning retailers have often said to me, "The only thing wrong with Birkenstocks is they last too long. I could sell a lot more if they broke down sooner!" Luckily, neither I nor Mr. Birkenstock gave in to that temptation. One of our core values was that quality would win out over price, and we trusted people would discover that quality is more economical in the long run. The look-alikes in the L.L.Bean catalog were inferior in quality: they weren't as durable, and they didn't provide the same benefits as Birkenstocks. It took a while for the public to realize this, but they finally returned to the "real thing." This experience with L.L.Bean reinforced my belief that the drive for "cheaper, cheaper, cheaper" is partly responsible for the economic messes like the one we are in right now. This concept can perhaps be most easily seen in the food industry: cheap food is produced with the help of subsidies so that the big outfits gain, but the organic farmer is struggling. This is an example of when Goliaths can harm not only the marketplace but also the individual.

Whenever something like this happened with the larger companies, the Goliaths, I wound up feeling okay about it because it brought me back to my own values. I believed in a quality product, and my heart was really with the smaller, independent retailers. I liked to nurture the smaller stores. I admired the store owners for their pluckiness and courage. They had to be multitalented in order to do everything the big stores did, including marketing, advertising, store design, and community relations. And they did it all with limited resources. It wasn't easy for them, so supporting them was a joy to me. In return, the smaller retailers remained loyal and dedicated to our product. Their values were aligned with ours, so they were a better fit for our company.

That philosophy paid off for us in the long run. Though some retail stores disappeared from the industry with consolidation, many of the specialty stores that carried Birkenstock remained. In the end, the "many small" outweighed the "one big." What a blessing that was.

Contracts Help You Get Clear

■ JOE, CREATIVE MACHINES

When you run a small business, you can sometimes have the illusion that a big job—the breakthrough job—is right around the corner and will assure everlasting success if you land it. In our business, when a big job like this comes along and there's a bunch of hype, everyone in the industry knows about it. One such project was the Experience Music Project, financed by Paul Allen in Seattle. A lot of companies were trying to get involved with it because it had a huge budget. The project was about rock 'n' roll, which is fun and cool. I worked on it a little bit, and it opened a few years later. It was okay, but then other jobs came along. I had more exhibits to build. Life went on. In this line of work, and maybe in other industries as well, no *one* job is going to push us over the edge and make us grow so much that we can think, "Now we've made it." That's an illusion that, as entrepreneurs, we have to get past.

The problem with growing very fast with one big job is that the growth is very expensive and difficult. By itself, growth is a full-time job. If we were really going to make a profit, it would probably not be one job that grew us really big because we would need every penny to get that big, and then our company would be poised for that level of growth. If another job of similar size didn't come along, we'd have a problem. A company like ours isn't very scalable. It isn't like we have ten people making widgets and if we had a hundred people we could make ten times the number of widgets. It's much more interdependent than that. Our staff has a unique mix of talents that isn't always transferable to another project.

Another form of Goliath is dealing with larger companies within the industry. I work in a small industry, and in some ways we're all dipping out of the same pot. I had a turning point a few years back, when I almost got in big trouble with a larger company in our industry. The experience taught me that business works best within a framework of contracts, letters of intent, the Uniform Commercial Code, and so on, all of which define a predictable sphere.

What happened was this: My company was paid by Company A to build some exhibit prototypes. We had a nondisclosure agreement saying we couldn't show the prototypes to anyone until they had been shown in public. But after that, they belonged to us, Creative Machines. We showed them in public and then when the opportunity arose to win an important job, we shipped these prototypes to Company B, where a prospective client was visiting. We were partnering with Company B to try to get a job with this client, and the prototypes would help the client see what kind of work we did. We were completely up front about the circumstances surrounding the prototypes—who designed them, who built them, who paid for them, and so on. What complicated matters was that Company A was trying to win the same job.

When the people at Company A found out we had used the prototypes that they had paid us to fabricate, they were angry. Company A's vice president called me and said, "Why did you do this? We're going to blacklist you." I replied, "I was very clear with the potential client what everyone's relationship was, and we had every contractual right to do this. We never misrepresented who designed what and who built what. The prototypes were ours to do with what we wanted by contract. We're allowed to display these publicly or do anything at all because the nondisclosure agreement is over." Saying this didn't calm the vice president. But as I was trying to explain my situation, I made a statement that changed everything. I said, "You can always count on me to act within the bounds of legality and ethics to advance the interests of my company, just like you would do for your business." After a long moment of silence, he spoke again and was relieved and satisfied with my response.

In a situation like this, irrationality and emotionality almost never works. A calm, level approach is much better. The person who had tipped off this vice president was very emotional. That scares other businesses. When I told the vice president that he could always count on me to further the interests of my business within the limits of legality and ethical behavior, he could understand because I was just another businessman like him. Company A has continued to work with us, and the guy who tipped off the vice president has never worked for that company again.

That's why I like contracts, up to a point. You definitely need them when your company starts to be big enough to deal with Goliaths. If you are relying on the other person's good feeling and emotion to keep your business relationship solid, what's to say that the emotion won't turn bad? I don't mean to say that if the other person is emotional you can't have a good business relationship, but you should have clearly defined rules, especially as your company gets bigger. Now, even for small jobs that I do for friends, I insist on a multipage letter of agreement so everyone is crystal clear about what is going to happen, and I can ultimately protect those relationships. The balance between business and friendships is especially important when you are dealing with Goliaths.

What We Learned

Dealing with Goliaths can feel scary, but these entrepreneurs lived to tell their Goliath tales, and so can you! Here are some things you might want to consider when a situation goes awry with a Goliath:

- *Understand the big picture.* Remind yourself that getting a sense of the long view is helpful but difficult to do in the middle of a tense situation. Try to take a step back and see that this moment is only one part of a very big picture. That might give you the strength and foresight to be able to pick up the pieces and take action.

- *Know your company and why you are running it.* Holding on to what makes our companies strong can get us through our encounters with Goliaths. When the going gets tough, pick up your product, read a rave customer review of your service, or reread your mission to remember the values that are your bedrock. This may sound hokey, but it helps.

- *Remember what you value most.* Knowing where you are willing to compromise and where you will not vary from your core values is the foundation of knowing who you are. Even if a Goliath promises to pick you up and take you to the next level, if you don't feel like you can adhere to your value system at the same time, then the ride might not be worth it.

- *Remind yourself that nobody goes it alone (sanely).* Another way to reconnect to the long view is to voice your fears and concerns to another business owner you can trust. On a day Lisa was facing multiple big issues—a key customer and a key employee wreaking havoc on the same day—she called a friend in distress, whining, "It's all a house of cards." Luckily, the friend had more perspective and big-company experience so he could say, "It's no problem really, Lisa. Even the biggest organizations feel like a house of cards." Rather than scaring her, these words helped her see that everything is a work in progress, and other businesses have similar problems. She wasn't as alone as she had thought.

- *Do it afraid if you have to; just make sure you do it.* Another way to say this is that when we feel like something is overwhelming, turn and face it. Many times the shadow thrown is much larger than the actual Goliath.

- *Know that many rivers lead to the ocean.* These stories teach us to find another way. Even if the alternative is not pretty, knowing that Goliath isn't the only option helps you to find another path out of the mess that dealing with Goliath might have created.

■ **PRACTICAL TIP**
Do Something Completely Silly
When you're feeling overwhelmed, do something that makes you giggle like a child. Make s'mores, jump in ocean waves, roll in a pile of leaves, finger-paint, play a practical joke on someone who will laugh, have a pillow fight, do your favorite card trick on an unsuspecting friend, or play the music of your teen years as loudly as you can stand and sing along.

Focus on the Next Step Only for the Next Hour

What is the one action you can take for the next sixty minutes that will address an issue in your company? Do that one action only for right now.

6

Facing forces beyond your control

Some of the most stressful times in business happen when our companies are at the mercy of much larger forces, such as cultural, economic, or cultural shifts we can't control. These shifts can include soaring interest rates, a diet trend, a fashion trend, a natural disaster, a frozen credit environment, a precipitous drop in consumer spending, or any change that makes it hard to find predictability. Sometimes customers and suppliers make big decisions or big mistakes that impact us, and even though we have done everything right and have remained true to our values, our company still suffers. Finding our way through this situation can be challenging and stressful.

In this chapter, entrepreneurs tell their stories about what happens when the trend is your friend and then it's not. Lisa tells the story of the low-carb diet trend that was a one-two punch to her company. Margot shares the effect that the dress-for-success fashion trend had on Birkenstock. Carol and Gary describe what happened when another company's decisions had serious consequences within their own businesses. And Joe tells the tale of a series of disasters that struck him all at the same time. At the end of the chapter, our practical tips give suggestions about how to get through tough times that you have absolutely no control over.

You Can Do *Anything,* But You Can't Do *Everything*

■ **LISA**

At Vermont Bread Company, one of the trends that caught us by surprise was that our customers began to rapidly consolidate. When we started selling natural and organic bread, there were a lot of independent stores, small supermarkets, and natural product chains. Over the years we steadily increased our capacity and followed a nice, smooth growth curve. Then, over the course of about a decade, the chains rapidly merged and became a handful of large supermarket retailers and one natural product chain. In a very short time we went from having a solid, multilegged stool of revenues to having only a very limited number of customers. Our size, relative to the size of these customers, became out of balance.

We needed to figure out how to increase our size in relation to these companies'. We needed a new idea. We noticed that supermarkets were using more upscale advertising and presentations, yet they continued to offer only what we called squishy white bread as their private-label products (the supermarket-brand bread). We thought it would be a good idea to develop a line of denser and higher quality breads that the supermarkets could put their names on. We called it a premium private label. It would be a small line but important for stores.

We were right: it was a good idea. But it didn't remain a small line. It grew to represent a significant amount of weekly volume at a premium price. Then a new low-carb diet craze hit. It was a tough time to be in a high-carb business, selling bread or pasta. Sales of flour-based products plunged. Within two years our industry's largest companies—the maker of Ronzoni pasta and the maker of Wonder Bread—had filed for Chapter 11 bankruptcy protection. When the larger bread companies saw that we were doing well with our premium private label, they decided to try to take this business away from us by offering something similar and being competitive on price. We believed our quality was higher, but we could not compete on price. Over a twelve-month period we would eventually lose most of our new business to these larger companies.

The first customer that decided to go with our large competitor was the only customer of significant size I had ever lost. At the time, this customer was an important leg of our multilegged stool of revenue. The news hit me like a punch in the gut. Immediately I pulled up the spreadsheet and looked at each week for the next two years. I erased the customer's sales line and ingredient costs. And then I started sweating because that change tipped us from profitability into the red. I went outside and walked around the building, hoping the fresh air might clear my head. I let myself feel the anger and frustration. I acknowledged the unfairness: we had built up business with this customer by trying a new idea, and now that it was successful, we lost the customer's business on price, not quality. I yelled and swore and kicked rocks as far as I could and yelled some more.

When I got back into my office, I looked at the spreadsheet again. Then I picked up the phone and called my bankers to tell them what had happened. I also told them I was updating the plan and would have something to present to them at the end of the week. Now I had a deadline! Next, I called in the key managers who would be involved in finding a solution. Together we brainstormed what changes we could make to bring us back into the black. We started to voice the real fear: that the rest of our private-label business would also be at risk once the marketplace knew that one customer had made the change. Luckily, we had two months left on the contract, so we had time to figure out what we would do. I spent sleepless nights worrying about what would happen if we lost more customers and how I could remain positive with our staff so we could work together to solve the problem. Over the next few weeks we found ways to cut expenses, open a new geographic territory for our branded products, and put off some new projects.

Getting through a crisis is about taking the next right step. Looking at everything that needs to get done at once can paralyze you, and you won't be able to do anything. A friend just sent me some feedback about the tips that are included in this book. He reminded me that you need to focus on the next right thing that matters most. You can do *anything*, but you can't do *everything*. When the low-carb trend hit, we knew that to keep our company healthy, sustainable, and focused on our core values, we had to get it back to profitability and ensure positive cash flow. Even as our business shrank for the first time in our history, we focused on these two goals and kept the blinders on. Eventually we found the path through the crisis—one loaf at a time.

The Trend Is Your Friend and Then It's Not

■ **MARGOT**

Many factors in our business were out of our control. The biggest one was the currency market. When I started importing Birkenstock sandals, this wasn't a problem because the value of the dollar against the German mark was fixed. Placing an order, we knew that the currency value would still be the same three months later when we received the merchandise and had to pay our bill. This was dependable. We could calculate our selling price and be sure of our margins.

A few years later, this security vanished overnight. For reasons that had to do with the world economy, the dollar was allowed to "float" against foreign currencies. It was traded like a commodity, and it fluctuated a lot between the time we ordered and the time we resold. Of course, we could not change our prices to the retailers: the consumer catalogs had been printed long before. We simply had to eat the difference, which could be as high as 20 percent. Sometimes we were lucky and the pendulum swung in our favor, but it was still a crazy situation. Talk about living with ambiguity! It was very unnerving, yet we learned how to adjust. We bought German mark futures in order to minimize risk—not a very stable solution, but what is stable in this world? The best we could do was to take a deep breath and go on with our work.

Fashion trends also affected our business and were out of our control. This is particularly important if you are dealing with apparel. When I started with Birkenstock, our sandals were totally unknown. Over time we gained a little foothold as people found out about us. Luckily, they were the right people: a large generation of baby boomers who were looking to change the world, were not interested in conforming, and wanted to look different from their parents. Birkenstock became their choice of footwear to express these values.

For almost eighteen years we grew as fast as we could manage and thought no end was in sight. If you don't have people to serve the customers, then you can't have any more customers, so we hired consultants, did strategic planning, and trained additional personnel for the growth that was coming our way. We kept busy, planning for the ongoing boom.

Quite suddenly, the landscape changed. "Dress for success" became the new motto, and making money was in. People were not wearing their Birks on the streets anymore. We had hired too many folks. We thought of asking people to volunteer to be laid off but decided against it because we were afraid we would lose our most valuable workers. We had to let people go, and it was terrible. It was agonizing trying to choose who would go and who could stay. I felt responsible for abandoning them in a cold world. A year or two later we would be able to rehire some of these people, which would make me feel a lot better, but I didn't know that then.

What helped us? Something that we held in our hearts the whole time: we knew we were not just a fashion trend. We had a solid foundation in our product and its benefits. At the time, a lot of people in the industry predicted this would be the end of the Birkenstock craze. The companies that had produced copies stopped making them and, though this was helpful in the long run, first they had to get rid of their inventory at sell-out prices. We struggled for quite a while before we could turn our ship around. Luckily, the people who had gotten used to comfort didn't want to give it up. Maybe they didn't wear the shoes to the office anymore, but they kept a pair under their desk and started to spread the word.

The whole episode taught me again that security doesn't exist. Situations can change overnight. Then again, many things you fear might happen, won't. For instance, I was afraid of bad press about our layoffs, but the local paper didn't print a word about them. Our reputation for being a good values-based company did not get damaged. I was grateful for that and promised myself once more to start worrying only *after* something bad happened and not before! Afterward, you can think about solutions to your problems, and that is far more productive than fretting about something that might never come about.

Another lesson I learned was not to suffer quietly within. I am an introspective type, and I didn't quite know how to open up and share my burden with the rest of the group. My long-time employee, Mary Jones, was my conscience in those days, and she pointed out that people would weather the crisis much better if they knew what was going on. I certainly agreed in principle, but due to my introverted makeup, it wasn't easy for me to get from theory to practice. With the help of a consultant, I managed to get up enough courage to share.

My first step was to have daily stand-up meetings with everybody in sales and marketing. We shared the ups and downs of what was happening. It was very unifying, and we kept it up for years. Later, the people in finance, IT, and operations wanted to participate in the meetings, too. By then the company had grown much bigger, and we could no longer get together every day. We settled on meeting every Friday at 11:30, just before lunch. Everyone was welcome to participate. Each department briefly shared what was happening within the company and out in the field. It widened people's perspectives and allowed us to see how we all fit together.

Though some good outcomes emerged from the shift in trends, dealing with the changes was still difficult. And when I look back, I would say what I found most helpful during that time was to take a wider perspective and ask some basic questions:

- What is changing?
- What seems to be emerging?
- What remains the same?
- What can we do to stem the tide?

In our case, what stayed the same was the basic shape of our sandals—we would not change that. What we could and did change was our marketing focus. We started to talk to the people who needed our shoes for medical reasons, were in standing occupations, and so on. We stopped saying we were "cool" and instead emphasized the health benefits. That gained us new loyal customers.

When Quality, Price, History, and Good Relationships Are Not Enough

■ CAROL, PUTNEY PASTA

When something is out of your control, when you are powerless to act against a changing business trend, it can be one of the hardest moments in running a business. The beginning of the end for my company happened when we lost our largest account. This story could have been told in the "Wrestling with Goliath" chapter, but I think it is interesting to focus on the fact that the reason we lost the account had to do with something that was completely out of our control: where we were located geographically.

For many years we serviced a West Coast–based private-label retail customer whose leaders loved our products, were aligned with our core values, appreciated our quality, and worked with us to increase the number of items we supplied them. Their orders grew every month. They paid their bills on time and were very pleasant to deal with. The company eventually represented 40 percent of our total business, and because of its growth we outgrew our original factory and had to move into a new plant, causing us to take on additional debt. When this company decided to expand to the East Coast, all of the east coast suppliers, including me, were ecstatic. I called Lisa Lorimer to say she should say yes to being the baked-goods supplier even if the company opened only a few stores. I told her that if she ever trusted me on anything, she should trust me on this. She had her doubts when the company had only three stores, but to this day she will call me and say, "Have I thanked you lately for that recommendation?" because this company eventually became her largest customer.

That expansion seemed to be such good news, but it triggered overall changes within the organization that wound up derailing our company. The customer's new East Coast team decided to source the bulk of their suppliers in the East. When the new West Coast buyers saw what folks on the East Coast were doing, they decided to do the same thing. They found new producers that were closer to their own stores out west. We understood their reasoning—they wanted to have shorter lead times so they could reduce their costs and be more responsive to the market—but it was painful for us because we were no longer their supplier. Suddenly our largest customer was gone. The company bought all the items we had ingredients and labels for, working with us for a smooth transition, but in a matter of a few short months my company's revenue was reduced by 40 percent. Our quality was terrific and consistent, our price was competitive, we had strong relationships with many people in the customer's organization, but that wasn't enough. Their decision was based solely on something that was out of our control—our geographic location.

It's true that we would have been better off if we'd had the multilegged stool mentioned earlier, but the point of this story is that sometimes there is nothing you can do about a decision being made within the industry, and you could lose your biggest customer because of it. If you want to know how this story ends, it is continued in chapter 9. Suffice it to say, it was the beginning of the end for Putney Pasta.

When Everything That Could Go Wrong Does Go Wrong

■ JOE, CREATIVE MACHINES

During the time my business was having serious financial problems because of our unsound business model, we were visited by a series of other problems that were completely out of our control. Two years before, we had installed a ten-thousand-kilowatt solar array to reduce our carbon footprint. We were the first private for-profit business in Tucson to do so, and suddenly, when energy prices soared, the media took notice of it. A news crew from the local television station climbed up on our roof and did a story about us. One week later I drove into work and saw that half our solar array had been stolen in the middle of the night. Everyone from the police to the insurance agency was mystified. Removing the panels was a lot of work, and they don't have much resale value. The television news crew promptly climbed back on the roof and did a follow-up story. The missing panels would cost about $40,000 to replace. Insurance paid for this eventually, but at the time the theft was a real blow.

A week or so later our drains stopped working. I walked outside our shop and saw a huge pit where the septic tank had been. That explained why the drains didn't work, but I didn't know why our septic tank would cave in all of a sudden. In general, when something breaks I try to replace it with something better—sort of how a broken bone heals with a thicker portion. I thought this would be a good time to connect to the county sewer line that ran just outside our property. I hired a contractor and rented a Porta Potti for a month. "After all," I thought, "how long could it possibly take to do the job?" I began the process of permitting, getting an easement, and so on, but the county was switching from one method of permitting to another and had added new requirements. There was also a hefty connection fee. Still, it seemed like the right thing to do. Looming in the back of my mind was the fact that the board of directors of our local art museum was planning to hold their annual meeting at our shop in three months' time. Surely the job would be finished by then.

As weeks went by without our receiving a permit, I started getting nervous. More weeks went by. I explained to our contractor, "These are wealthy patrons of the arts. They'll be dressed in suits and a lot of alcohol will be served. I can't ask them to use a Porta Potti." But the matter was out of his hands. I would have worried more, except that I was busy dealing with other problems: replacing the stolen solar array, borrowing money to stay afloat, retooling our business model, dealing with a slew of bad warranty issues, and trying to fill the shoes of an outstanding employee who had left. I didn't have time to worry about a bathroom for the board of directors. As soon as one problem was solved, another arose: our compressor broke down, one of our buildings flooded, our laser cutter quit working, and so on. It felt like we were being visited by a series of biblical plagues.

Through it all, my employees commiserated and watched closely how I responded, and I told anyone who was listening that it is easy to pretend you know what you are doing when you are successful but that true greatness comes from how you handle adversity. I had trouble sleeping; it became the worst year of my life. Still, I never considered giving up. I didn't consider failure an option. I had been working at the business too long for that. And I really believed that how I handled adversity was more important than how I had handled success in the past or would handle success in the future.

None of these grand thoughts helped push the county to approve our permit for the sewer hookup. The date for the big directors' meeting and party loomed closer. Finally my contractor, who was an earthy sort of guy, came up with a solution. He would simply dig a pit with his backhoe in the location where the sewer pipe had broken off, install a temporary sewage container, cover the pit with plywood and dirt, and no one would be the wiser. The board members would still essentially be using a Porta Potti but it would all look like a standard toilet so it would seem civilized. No one would have to know.

The party was a great success. The board members played with all our exhibits and art pieces; they shot our tennis ball cannon; they had a lot to drink. Years later, influential people in Tucson still come up to me and say how much they enjoyed that party. I smile when I think of our secret solution to the septic tank problem.

Somehow, being able to solve that problem marked the beginning of the turnaround. We got the solar array replaced. We bought a better compressor. We fixed our warranty issues. My employees came together as a team and became stronger than when we had depended so much on that one outstanding employee. I changed our business model. It took a lot of hard work with no end in sight, but the event I'll remember most of all was the septic tank cave-in and the weird solution of digging a pit so everything could appear normal until it actually became normal.

Dealing with a Foreclosure with a Ball and a Racquet

■ **GARY, STONYFIELD FARM**

My best advice about dealing with crises is to first be sure that you are taking care of yourself. This means sleeping and eating well and being sure that you are getting away from your work. For instance, I have learned that I can't make good decisions unless I exercise. Even in the midst of a deep financial or personnel crisis, I often take a walk, jump on a bike, head off to the woods to ski, or play tennis. Often the right answer comes to me when I put the problem away and my heart is pumping. I cannot remember a single instance when I didn't have better judgment after exercising than I had before stepping away for a break.

I learned this lesson in the early, fragile days of our business. We had exceeded the capacity of our little hilltop farm and had begun producing our yogurts at a friend's dairy in western

Massachusetts. Late one night, we were told by his banker that a foreclosure of the dairy was imminent. Early the next morning, the bank pulled the plug, and we found ourselves with no production facility, no cash, and the need to absorb the failed firm's huge debts. Panicked, we began to make all kinds of crazy plans and started the phone calls to follow them up. By 10 that evening, we had crafted a completely convoluted scheme to take over the dairy's obligations. As soon as I could secure the cash, we could restart operations. But something wasn't sitting right with me. In fact, I was feeling a bit ill. So I called a friend, and we went out to hit some tennis balls at a nearby club. (The club offered free court time at 10:00 p.m. on weekdays.)

The right path came to me, partly because I had stepped away from the war room and partly, I am sure, because I got my heart pumping and my endorphins kicking in. As my friend and I began to warm up in that empty, semidark, cavernous place, I felt a lump welling up inside. As I hit the balls harder and harder, that lump became a steady stream of tears. Each time I whacked a fuzzy ball, another sob burst out. I still have no idea if my opponent ever realized what was happening to me that night, but through this cathartic release of tension, I shed something else besides tears. I abandoned the completely crazy scheme we'd hatched in favor of something much more sane: "getting out of Dodge."

The next morning, we walked away from the failed dairy and its bank and headed off on our own. Thirteen months later, after dragging ourselves through a nightmarish period of trying to keep up with demand at our original little dairy farm, we opened our brand-new Yogurt Works. We became profitable and have grown and existed happily ever since. It all began on that tennis court with the clarity that for me comes only from burning some calories, getting out of my head, and letting my juices flow.

What We Learned

For most of us who ran established values-driven businesses, economic and cultural trends worked in our favor as we developed new products, grew into wider markets, and hired more staff. We were able to focus on people, the planet, and profits and the trend was our friend. But inevitably, trends shift, and many of the old ways won't work any more. The economy might slow down, funding for new projects can get put on hold, fashions can move from casual to dress-for-success, or a new diet craze can sweep the country. Decisions by customers and suppliers can impact your business even when you think you have done everything right. Below are some ideas for dealing with the tough stuff that is out of your control.

- *Face it squarely.* Ignoring a changing trend or burying your head in the sand won't help. Try to see the new trend as quickly and clearly as possible. If you wake up at 3:00 a.m. because of worries about employees, cash, or a big screwup that might have legal implications, wait until morning. When the sun rises, you'll be able to take a deep breath and see your problem in a new light so that you can face it and put one foot in front of the other.

- *Remember, this too shall pass.* It is easy to think that whatever is happening now will always be happening. It won't. We can't ignore the first tip, but it is important to remember the trend will eventually shift again. You will figure out how to deal with the natural disaster or the customer decision that put you in a tailspin.

- *Go back to the basics.* When dealing with a crisis, it helps to stick with pragmatics. You might ask yourself how you can you tighten your belt, eliminate expenses, drive new sales in new channels, collect cash sooner, negotiate better terms with your suppliers, increase your efficiencies, or term out your debt with longer amortizations.

- *Convene the advisory board.* Now is the time to schedule an extra advisory board meeting. Get that A-team assembled to help you think in new ways.

- *Do the research.* Try to see what is happening as clearly as possible. For example, the low-carb diet craze put big bread and pasta companies into bankruptcy. But anyone buying the diet books and doing the research would have seen that a focus on whole grains would fit into these new diets.

- *Ask yourself questions.* When things feel out of control, ask yourself,

  - What changes can I make to find a niche in the landscape of this changing economy?
  - What products or services will my customers need that are similar to what I offer now?
  - How can I increase my cash flow during this time?
  - What would make my company more profitable right now?
  - How can I change the delivery of what our company offers?
  - What creative and funny guerrilla marketing campaign could we run? For instance, during the recent economic downturn, the owner of a painting contracting firm came up with the campaign "Will Work for Food," in which she combined her commitment to supporting the local food bank with a play on the difficult economic times. What can work in your business?
  - What can I do to take care of myself? Gary liked hitting a tennis ball as hard as he could. What works for you?

■ PRACTICAL TIP

**Consciously Make Space Away from the Work
(Even If You Are at Work)**

Start with just fifteen minutes: turn off the phone and the computer, close the door, and imagine a big trunk outside the office door where you put all your thoughts about the business—they will still be there when you are done. Every time a thought comes into your head, imagine it floating out and landing in the trunk. Then consciously relax each part of your body. Tell yourself to relax your toes, then the bottoms of your feet, then your ankles—do this all the way up to your brain. In your business you focus on profit, planet, and *people*—remember, one of those people is *you*.

■ PRACTICAL TIP

Do What Matters

You can do anything, but you can't do everything. Looking at everything that needs to be done at once can paralyze you. Focus on the next action that matters most—getting through a crisis is about taking the next right step.

7

Managing your mistakes

We have talked about some of the tough stuff that happens in values-driven businesses: trends that turn against us, problem customers, the loss of employees, and a lack of cash, to name a few. But sometimes we just plain screw up or base our decisions on poor judgment. Especially frustrating are the times that we are convinced we are doing the right thing for all the right, socially responsible reasons and we still mess up.

In this chapter, Lisa describes getting a wake-up call when two of her employees got into a fistfight. Margot tells us two stories: one about the early days, when she printed too many catalogs, and a second one about an employee issue that ended in a lawsuit. Gary writes about a manufacturing mess-up, and Joe explains how he made a core mistake in finding a sustainable way to keep his company running.

In this chapter, we tell the truth about those times we made mistakes and had no one to blame but ourselves. What works best during these times is to acknowledge that a mistake was made and work on how we might be able to make better judgment calls in the future.

Missing the Obvious: Addressing the Emotional Side of Change

■ **LISA**

One of my biggest screwups was an automation project we did at Vermont Bread Company. I actually use the story as part of a presentation I do for Rotary clubs and chambers of commerce, titled "All the Things We Messed Up in Our Automation Project." One of the main issues I had to face during this time was my own arrogance—especially the Socially Responsible Mindset Arrogance. (I hate that!)

For years we had been dealing with the symptom of high turnover in our production department at the bakery. We tried all kinds of fixes: changing schedules, working only four days a week, and implementing a new benefit system, but the real problem was the work itself. It was hot, physical, brutal work. You really had to be either an eighteen- to twenty-four-year-old male or a rare woman with incredible upper-body strength to work with us. When a young woman friend of mine, who was an athlete and a runner, needed work for a few weeks, she asked me for a job. A day and a half into it, she was in tears. She told us it was impossible to do the work. At that point, I knew we really needed to deal with the root of the problem: we needed to automate our plant. Then we could actually adhere to our values and have a diverse workforce. People would be able to work at the bakery until retirement. So we started on the path to automation.

In the middle of the automation project, a bunch of people were working late to install equipment. I was in my office and heard loud voices down the hall. I figured the techs were listening to Rush Limbaugh and had turned up the radio, but the noise kept getting louder and louder. When I went into the hallway to ask them to turn down the radio, the door of the production office burst open and two of my key employees came tumbling out, screaming at each other. A fistfight had started.

A smaller, obvious lesson I learned that day was that men in fistfights do not hear women's voices. I ran into the bakery to get my male business partner to break up the fight. Once the combatants were separated, one of the employees could not calm down. His face was red, and he started screaming at my business partner and me. He called us liars and said he was sick of us playing games with him. Nothing we said calmed him down. Until that moment, I would have defined this man as one of our steadiest, calmest, most reliable workers. We eventually told him to go home, said we would pay him for his shift, and asked him to come back when he was a lot calmer.

I was floored, I thought we had this project licked; I thought I had done everything right. The whole process had been very values oriented and socially responsible. We had meetings about retaining employees, we had staff discussions about automation, and we all looked at equipment brochures together. I showed videos, put pictures and layouts on the break-room table, took people on field trips to other automated plants, and brought thirteen people to a bakery show in Las Vegas. We had been so proud of ourselves. What we hadn't taken into account was how we had completely changed the world of Vermont Bread Company.

In the next few days I spent a lot of time talking with my friends and other business owners about what was happening. I began to understand that even though the work promised to be easier and we would have a chance to be fully staffed more often, I had fundamentally changed the employees' lives. We hadn't just changed the machines, we had changed all of our mental processes as well. Before the automation project, we had three teams that each solved their own problems and then passed the product onto the next team. Now those three teams would be consolidated into one big team. People wouldn't be able to solve a single problem without understanding the entire system. This scared some of the employees. They knew how to do their jobs, and they were good at them. They got a lot of positive feedback on their skills. They had young families, new mortgages, and car payments. They made livable wages at the bakery and had good benefits. Even though we told them their jobs would be easier with automation and they would be able to learn how to use the new equipment, it didn't matter. It was a change. It was computerized. And it was scary. Most of all, despite the appearance of cooperation and shared information, the change was my choice and it was under my control, not theirs.

As happens with a lot of mistakes, I started out with really good intentions. We thought we were treating the root cause of a problem rather than the symptoms by following the path of making the work more appropriate for a diverse workforce, but we came to realize the root system was much more tangled than we initially thought. In order to untangle that root system, we had to ask for help. Before the automation project, representatives from a local employee assistance program had called a number of times to ask if I would like to make use of their services. I had never signed up. I thought we didn't need them. But after the fight happened, I found the number and called. Basically I said, "Okay, now I understand why you are in the world. Please come and help me."

The good thing about screwing up is that I learned from it. I could use the information to do better next time. A few years later, when we were in the middle of implementing an integrated computer system, I was able to look back on the automation project. I remembered the lesson I learned before about how huge the impact of such a change could be, and I was able to give the staff the support they needed through the company-wide changes.

So much of the learning and relearning we do when we screw up is figuring out how to recognize and deal with fundamental change. When you are in the midst of it, you might feel like you are on a roller coaster. Well, the truth is, you are. And rather than get nervous about how you might screw up, you can laugh and say, "Oh yeah, here we are on that roller coaster again!"

Mail Order and the Time-Saving Technique of Settling Out of Court

■ **MARGOT**

The first time I screwed up was pretty soon after I started the business. Mr. Birkenstock realized we were struggling to get stores to carry the sandals and explained how he got Birkenstock off the ground in Germany. He had read a book titled *How I Made a Fortune in Mail Order*, and its advice had worked for him. So in 1968 I translated his German catalog into English, bought one hundred thousand copies, and had them shipped to the United States. We rented mailing lists for health enthusiasts, but since we had more catalogs than we could afford to mail out, I sent two thousand at a time. It was a disaster. We did sell some shoes, but I got more back with a request for a refund than I ever mailed out. The letters went something like this: "You can't expect me to wear those. My husband says they look like gunboats!" We had those catalogs for years to come; some even traveled with me to our new warehouse in San Rafael. The prices had changed by that time, but the pictures were still valid. We kept using them for years. We just pasted over the old price list with the latest prices.

The screwup was trying to follow someone else's business plan. The difference between our mail-order campaign and Mr. Birkenstock's was that by sheer luck he had hit on the right list for him. He had mailed the catalogs to all the physicians in Germany. They understood the orthopedic value of the shoes. They bought them for their own use, paid full retail, and recommended them to their patients. It couldn't have been better for Mr. Birkenstock, but it sure didn't work for us. What worked for us was far more time-consuming—the slow, patient effort of explaining the sandals to one person at a time. I went to conventions, health fairs, anywhere I might find people who would be interested. Pretty soon our early retailers did the same, spreading the word to their communities and putting us on the road to success.

My next painful screwup came a few years later, when we had sales of about $1.2 million. Our organization was pretty loose at the time. With our expanding sales, I knew we had to tighten up, but I didn't know how. I found a consultant who had developed a system for organizing a company. It was a lengthy process. He studied our business, interviewed our employees, and then asked three of them and me to come to his office so he could unveil his plan. Without telling me beforehand, he named one of our employees the head of marketing. I really couldn't see her in that position, but I didn't have the guts to stop it right then and there. I also thought that perhaps he could see something in her that I couldn't, so I let it slide.

It soon became clear that the woman was in way over her head and couldn't do the job. I stopped using this consultant, and I fired the woman. However, she filed a lawsuit. I had to get an attorney. The way this kind of litigation works is crazy: her attorney conducted a deposition and my attorney conducted a deposition, and both went on for hours. I felt this was very unproductive and took far too much time and energy.

Believing there was a better way to handle disputes, I found out about mediation. At the time, only one attorney in our county practiced mediation. My employee was willing to meet with this attorney, so we had a very frank talk and settled the matter. In other words, I paid her off. My original attorney was furious. He was sure I would have won the case, and he was afraid I would get a reputation for settling with people and would be sued again. I was willing to take that risk, and I never was sued again because I learned how to act better in the future. I felt guilty—after all, the consultant had put the woman in that position; she had never applied for it. And I had allowed it to happen. It was more truthful to apologize and pay. It also saved a lot of time that could be put to better use!

I found out that the most important action to take when I do screw up is to admit it, not to defend my actions in order to save face. First, I try to forgive myself. Then I listen to my insides—"What feels right?"—and I act on that. In the aftermath of a major mistake, a person can get quite scared, afraid of screwing up again. But being paralyzed does not help the business. Especially in these uncertain times, we need all the courage we can muster to come up with new and untried solutions. It's one of life's paradoxes. Only experience can teach us how far to go in either direction. If it happens that something doesn't work out, we can forgive ourselves, keep our sense of self-worth intact, realize that we learned a lot, and go on with confidence.

If You Build It, They Will Come

■ **GARY, STONYFIELD FARM**

We've screwed up plenty in all facets of the company. I've had to cut my losses with hiring. I've had marketing efforts that just weren't right. We've conceived of all kinds of crazy things—from garden salad yogurt to something that was perhaps the right product at the wrong time. Sometimes it is impossible to make the right choice and you have to live with that. This can happen when you make a decision too fast. Sometimes I have approved something in a hurry and then woken up in the middle of the night, realizing it wasn't right and that it could cost us a lot of money. At the same time, you can't delay decisions in business or you could lose out.

My biggest problems in business have been the ones I created. No one else was responsible for them. I couldn't blame the market, the money situation, other people, or anything else. I have had my share of challenges in terms of not having enough money or not having it when I needed it or maybe trusting the wrong person, but whatever the problem was, I learned to stop pointing fingers. Eventually I had to look in the mirror and see my own role in it.

When I started out, though, screwing up involved thinking it was anyone else's responsibility but mine. I used to feel resentment toward people who wouldn't invest money in my company or donate money to it. I felt critical of people who would say they were socially responsible but then wouldn't step up to the plate. I would say, "Look, here we are doing all this stuff that is exactly what you said you were looking for, yet you are not investing in it." But now I realize that it's too easy to say, "Oh, those damn investors." In fact, the entrepreneur is responsible for selling his own idea and selling it well. The entrepreneur needs to be able to make a really clear case for why investors should want to put their money into it. If you have a good thing and you are able to make a good case for it, then *if you build it properly, they will come.*

Once my company was off the ground, big mistakes happened when I made decisions I wasn't qualified to make. I didn't recognize my own limitations. When I think back to some of my learning, this was one of the biggest lessons for me. For instance, I went off to manufacture in Russia. From an entrepreneurial point of view, a relatively logical set of decisions led me to think we should manufacture there, but my CFO was aghast. We were just coming into our own. We were running a $40 million company and we had so much going on. She saw the Russian venture as a huge, huge waste of my time, and she felt like it was a distraction in terms of our investment money. It took me a year and half to realize my CFO was right. We lost $750,000 in the process, and I almost lost my life. I got into these mafia situations with Uzis, and the whole thing was pretty hairy. That mistake, even though it was a doozy, really expanded my personal listening. I also realized that I was unqualified to make that decision in the first place.

From this experience, I understood that my pathological optimistic self could sow the seeds of our undoing. I've gone forward with other new ventures, and I still am pathologically optimistic, but now I check my ideas out with other people before I act on them. I learned through that. I learned what I'm not. I learned it's okay to accept my limitations and ask for help. I've learned to be less stubborn and willing to let go of things that aren't working, whether that's a product or something else. I keep little reminders around about errors we made so that I can learn from them. The idea is to try to shorten the learning curve.

One of the challenges of growth is that with a $300 million company, the costs of wrong or delayed decisions are much bigger, and the number of lives that are affected is greater. A company goes through growth stages, from the child to the adolescent to the grown-up. In some respects, adolescence is a good time to work this stuff out because you can make mistakes that are a lot less expensive, even though at the time you might think that nothing could be bigger. But if you are successful with these small decisions, you *will* get bigger, so you might as well learn when you are small.

Losing an Employee and the Flawed Business Model

■ JOE, CREATIVE MACHINES

Last year was probably the worst year ever, and I think it was because of two major screwups. The first one was that we had a fundamentally flawed business model: we did only custom work. We had somehow been lucky enough to survive for more than ten years with only custom work, but during this year I realized that all it would take was a few mistakes, and we would fail irreparably. We had gotten ourselves into a situation where we had nothing to fall back on. I found myself taking exhibit jobs I really didn't like just to make enough gross sales to keep everyone employed.

In order to fix this screwup I needed a steady moneymaker for my business. I didn't want the moneymaker to take a lot of time, and I didn't want it to be useless. I didn't want to make poodle collars or avocado slicers, for example. That's where the socially responsible piece comes in for me. I wanted to make something useful that engaged the mind. At about the time I was realizing this, I lost one of my best employees, which was a wake-up call. The truth was, I wasn't paying him as much as I should have been. This employee had been with us from the beginning. When he said he had to leave, I said, "I feel bad because you've really helped build this company. In a bigger company, you'd have equity. You'd have some ownership. In my mind, you *do* have ownership. I have always intended to reward all your early work with a much higher salary as soon as possible." He said, "Well, you've done a lot for me, but I don't know how you can keep that promise." He didn't speak harshly, but he was a little negative. I don't think he believed that the situation could really change.

Even though I couldn't have paid more at the time, I could have been paying attention to his morale as an employee of Creative Machines. He handled a lot of tough jobs, which I didn't appreciate until later. He would go on trips for installations and build exhibits. If any warranty issues came up, he would feel responsible for them. But he was rarely able to see the successes. When you're building, you're dealing with the client, and that can be a hassle—especially while you're in the process of the installation. Afterward, you hear only about the problems the exhibit has. You tend to overlook the fact that in between the problems, hundreds of thousands of people are enjoying the exhibit you built. My employee didn't see that enough, and I don't think I gave him enough chances to experience it. I've worked in museums, so I know how much enjoyment people get out of the exhibits, but if you haven't worked in museums, you might not get that kind of gratification.

This employee happened to leave at the same time I was realizing the way we were operating wasn't working, we were running out of money, and it felt like things were crashing in around me. Then I got a call from Rock Stream Studios, which made ball-machine sculptures. The owner of the business wanted to retire. For years he'd been selling ball-machine sculptures all over the world, and he wanted to sell the company. The demand for the ball-machine structure continues, and they offer a huge profit margin. They're sold as individual custom art pieces, and no two are identical, but they're easy to fabricate because they're very similar to one another. They share most mechanisms, and the ball can go through a menu of a hundred actions: it hits the cow bell and the cow kicks it; it lands in a little walk and then goes to a Ferris wheel, hits three frogs, and goes into the cow's mouth; and so on. All the details, such as what parts to use, what bearings, and what spacing, have been worked out. I can hand a project off to employees and it gets done without demanding a lot of brain power. I like working on that kind of stuff. It's fun to work on a project you know will be appreciated and you're fairly sure will succeed.

Now that we have the ball-machine sculptures as a constant moneymaker, we don't have a flawed business model anymore. We're not out of the woods yet—I am still searching for something else that can supply regular income—but we are doing much better. If we'd had a steady moneymaker earlier, I might have had more cash on hand, and that key employee might never have left. He got a well-paying job in his hometown. He visited the shop a while ago, and he seemed good. Ironically, now that Creative Machines is doing better, I could have paid him a lot more. But if those screwups hadn't happened, I might not have learned about how a consistent moneymaker can help in all facets of business—from paying a key employee well to making more creative work.

I have to remember that screwups are part of what it means to run a company, and though we've come close to failing, and it may happen again, we can learn from our mistakes. All creativity, in one sense or another, is about managing failure. The creative process has more dead ends than open doors. So the questions become, How do I learn from my mistakes so I don't make them again? How do I stop them before they damage me too much? You can learn a lot from a screwup, but it can feel scary to make mistakes. When you hear or read stories of people who have done really well, you find out the difference between them and someone who failed was that they were able to withstand their mistakes. The bad times didn't get to them.

They were able to continue. They might have felt like failures but they kept getting up and doing it again. In a way, a small business like mine is about managing failure. It's about carrying on when you do screw up.

What We Learned

We could tell plenty of other stories about the mistakes we've made over the years. The point is that sometimes we just blow it. No big trends affect us, no Goliaths overwhelm us, no employees make bad decisions—we just screw up, pure and simple. So what do we do when we make a mistake?

- *Face it.* The mess-up starts to get fixed as soon as we can turn our attention toward it and try to see it clearly. For many of us, that first "taking our head out of the sand" is the most difficult step. But once we face the mistake, we can start to fix it.

- *Own it.* Mistakes can be particularly irritating when we think we have done everything the right way. We have considered not only the success of the company but also the people who work for us and the environment in which we live. We have been inclusive in our process and transparent in our actions. Yet we still screw up. We just have to own it and move on.

- *Get the help you need to move through it.* Whether you can contact your advisory board, an employee assistance program, or a consultant, make sure you talk out the problem so that you won't be as liable to make the mistake again. Fix what can be fixed, hope you have learned from the situation, and get up tomorrow morning and start again.

Remember to Write Down All of the Positive Things That Have Happened This Week

Have a notebook that lists just the good stuff, such as accomplishments and finished projects. Use it as a resource for building confidence and remembering that you don't always screw up!

Get a Massage or Manicure or Haircut or Shave

Even if you bite your nails, start today to get them in shape. Or take an hour and finally get that massage you've promised yourself. The times when you are hardest on yourself are also the times when you need to be the nicest to yourself!

8

Playing president

Not every entrepreneur agrees on what it means to play the role of president within our companies, but every one of us has had to wrestle with the concept. At business conferences, people talk about how to integrate that role with our personal lives. Do you ever wonder how that can even be possible? Can you really be your authentic self in all parts of your life? And which self, which role, is the authentic one anyway? The leader of a values-driven business ultimately has decision-making power that nobody else in the company has, so this role is fundamentally different from most of the other roles we play in our lives, whether it be spouse, partner, friend, board member, volunteer, parent, or child.

This chapter is about learning how to bring the values of collaboration, respect, and diversity into that leadership role. Lisa reminds us not to compare our insides with everyone else's outsides. Margot describes the changes that happened over time in her role as president and how, even today, her role as a "legend" still impacts her life. Joe talks about times when the stress of owning a company felt overwhelming and he was tempted to work for someone else so that he wouldn't have to handle all the responsibility. Marie reminds us that the role of president is intricately woven with the mission of our organizations. Carol describes the internal disconnect that can happen when you are struggling in your business and personal life but you have to project the image of a successful businessperson to the outside world. Finally, Tom talks frankly about how the pressure of his role brought him to the brink of burnout and what he did to bring himself back.

Comparing Your Insides with Other People's Outsides

■ LISA

The strange phenomenon of owning a company was that my authentic self was much different from the role I played as president. Playing president was odd for me because I was a very private person. I never wanted to talk about my personal life at work. I was in a long-term relationship, but none of my customers, distributors, or suppliers knew that. Some of my employees eventually knew, but my partner never came to the bakery. I also had to be much more outgoing than I usually am, much more engaged in what people had to say. Had I not headed a company, I would have spent a lot less time with people. I would have been off in a corner reading more. I would have unplugged the phone. You can't do that if you are president. You feel a lot of pressure to be friendly. Employees look to you to be in a good mood, and if you aren't, it's upsetting to everyone.

When you are president, you are not really considered a person; you represent power. You have the power to change lives dramatically since forty to fifty hours of your employees' time is spent in the workplace. Tiny decisions you make affect their lives. In a way, you can't really have an equal and healthy relationship with them. When employees came into my office, I could feel that they were not speaking with me, Lisa Lorimer; they were speaking to a character, my role. Sometimes they would come at me in a combative way, and I knew they would never do that if they remembered I was a human being. Somewhere along the way you have to acknowledge that you don't have an equal relationship.

The struggle is that whenever you are out of your house, whether in the office or not, you may feel like you have to continue playing the role. You have to walk down the street in a bubble like a celebrity (but on a smaller scale). Because of this, sometimes you may cross the line and forget that you have an authentic self. This happened to a fellow CEO whose company was struggling. She was serving on a board, and she felt she had nothing to say, no advice to give, because her company wasn't doing well. She forgot that she had a voice separate from her company.

Because we have to play this role both in our companies and in our communities, a disconnect often happens between what is going on inside us and what we are projecting to the world. Our outsides don't necessarily match our insides. It may look as though we are doing well on the outside—we are profitable, we are selling like mad, we can't keep up with the amount of orders, we smile and nod and look superconfident—but inside we are feeling stressed and panicked.

This point was driven home to me when I was at a retreat center at one of the Social Venture Institutes in Hollyhock, British Columbia. These institutes bring together seasoned entrepreneurs with second- and third-stage company leaders so they can do case studies and have blocks of time together for problem solving and skill building. One of the best parts of the event is in the evening, after dinner, when a leader of a larger company tells his or her story in all its messy glory. It used to be known by the war metaphor "Tales from the Trenches," but it is now called "True Confessions." It involves telling the whole story, not the public-relations-approved story—no holds barred, no commercials allowed.

I met a man at this event who allowed me to understand the facades we put up as business leaders. As CEO of an interesting food company, he was trying to raise money for growth capital, and he had told his story during one of the sessions. I asked him to take a walk with me because I wanted to know more about what he was doing. While we were on the trail, I quizzed him about his sales, his distribution, how many employees he had, what his production facility was like, how he sourced his raw material, and what his margins were. He was in a classic phase of growing his company. I knew that behind his story, a lot of other things were probably happening. I imagined his sales were increasing and quickly gobbling up all his cash. He'd most likely outgrown his long-term staff and his communication systems. He probably needed more structure. And all the while he was having to present a solid image to the public so he could raise the money he needed to create a stronger internal team to attract more customers. When he finished telling me about his business, I shook my head and laughed: "Your life absolutely sucks right now. I remember being that size. It is so hard. You are growing so fast, nothing works like it used to, and the outside world thinks everything is going great because you have to put a game face on all the time. Yuck." Before I had finished talking, the man burst into tears.

We are all trying to act like everything is fine on the outside even if it's not. As CEO or president, you have to act like that. But that means we never really know that other business leaders are going through exactly the same things we are. A few years ago, I attended the three-year Owner/President Management Program at Harvard Business School. At that time, I was CEO of the largest woman-owned manufacturing company in Vermont, one of the top ten fastest growing businesses in the state. I was being sought out for my advice on legislative issues, hosting business groups, giving graduation speeches, and serving on boards, yet I hadn't cashed a full paycheck for months. My role was a cloak that I put on. My class had 156 students from all over the world. We were all owners and presidents of $10 million to $100 million dollar companies. On the third day of class, while we were doing a case study, our professor looked at us and asked, "So are you done being intimidated by everyone else in the class yet?" We all laughed. Then we paused. Then we laughed again even louder. It sank in that each of us was as intimidated by the others as they were of us. We were all business owners who had to say, "Great! I'm doing great!" even if things were going horribly.

In order to attract investors and employees, a company needs to project the image of success. Success breeds success. On a more personal level, the only place you can get a positive performance review when you are the owner of a private company is from the world. You know all the bad stuff, but you don't want to spread it around; you want what is good about you to be reflected in the eyes of the world and this can be stressful.

Every part of you is affected by that stress when you are president of the company. Not only do problems occupy the mind; they occupy the body. It wasn't until I sold my company that I understood how much my body had been affected by what went on. When I was no longer president, I heard about something big that happened at Vermont Bread Company, and for the first time, I couldn't *feel* the news. The problem occupied my mind only. I saw it as an interesting business challenge. As president, whenever I got bad news in my company, I felt my face turn red and my ears go hot. I felt the news go through me like fire. This was true especially when it was a big piece of information, like when an employee cut off the top of his finger on my equipment. I was standing on my deck at home when I got the call, and a strong feeling coursed through my body. Then I fainted.

Issues like this wreaked such havoc on my body that I had a heck of a time falling asleep at night. My trick during these difficult times was to become quite good at hitting a softball. I had read somewhere about an experiment done with athletes. One group practiced their particular skill regularly on the field and another group used only visualization. The group that used visualization actually performed equal to or better than the other group. So every night as I was trying to fall asleep, I spent hours visualizing hitting a softball. (I became a good hitter for my league team during the next season!) When I had batting practice at night while I fell asleep, I also started to realize a really important fact about my role as president: I couldn't do it alone.

As president, I needed people to talk to. My original business partner had left, and our thirteen-year conversation had left with him. Bringing my problems home wasn't an option because, though my family could love me and be empathetic, they couldn't really help me. Usually I just dumped my problems in an imaginary urn before I went in the front door at night and tried to leave them all behind. At work, I was head honcho and supposedly had everything under control, so I couldn't talk to anyone there. Where was I supposed to get support? I tried Rotary and the chamber of commerce and immediately ran home again. That's when I decided to set up my first advisory board. I chose strong people who could stand up to me, and I brought them together three to four times a year. I would get a room at the Putney Inn, and we would meet for discussion and dinner. It was such a gift to have a place to cry, plan, and try new ideas. When I outgrew the first group, I put my Business-Owner Queen's crown on again and fired them nicely and brought in a new group. Those boards got me through the good times and the bad—and had fun doing it.

It is helpful to have an advisory board, but even so, trying to project a positive image to the world and pretend that everything is going well can be difficult, and over the long haul that stress can get very hard to handle. Not only can it be stressful for the business owner, but it can also be stressful to the people around her. We all know about the stress of dealing with difficult people: the customer who calls with threats to cut off your sales, the talented employee who acts out in the workplace, the vendor who overpromises and underperforms. I had years of experience and various strategies for effectively addressing these difficult people. What I wasn't prepared for was when that person with the bad attitude at work—in my company, on my payroll—was me.

I had been running Vermont Bread Company for most of my adult life. We strived to incorporate our values into the workplace—respect and fairness, quality and integrity—and we always managed with an open door, but a year and a half before I stepped down as president, I shut that open door. I was cranky, short-tempered, miserable, unsmiling, and exhausted. I was stressed out from trying to play the role of president. Finally, I had to stop.

Of course, we all get burned out, stressed, and overwhelmed at various times in our lives, and we don't always have to step down, but we do have to look at our power roles, including where we might be abusing them and where we are toxic. It is a good idea to communicate with someone who can help. Hiding from something doesn't make it go away. After fessing up to feeling stressed and overwhelmed, we can begin to figure out how to take care of ourselves. Each of us is playing a role—it's part and parcel of what it means to grow a company. You can never know what is behind a role, so never compare your insides to someone else's outsides. And never forget your authentic self: feed her, water her, and take care of her.

On Being the Servant and the Master

■ **MARGOT**

For me, the title "president" was only a word on the incorporation papers when I started out. When only three people were working for Birkenstock, we were all in it together, and I didn't feel like I was playing a role. I didn't have time to think about it because work needed to be done—the phone needed to be answered, letters had to go out, and shoes had to be packed. I was involved with every part of the business, from getting the word out to getting the product out. Later, I realized I had to leave much of the daily nitty-gritty to others and concentrate on building the company. That's when the role of president started. The employees pushed me into it. They had expectations and notions of what it meant to be president.

By the time the company grew to two hundred employees, a lot of hierarchies had built up. Supervisors weren't supposed to talk to people who were twice removed from their positions because the managers might feel the supervisors were going behind their backs. This didn't happen consciously; people were just playing their roles within the fabric of the company. I didn't really honor "rules" like this, but I never felt I was getting to know the true person when I spoke to an employee. Certain natural barriers existed between us. Employees wanted to put on a good front. They did this unintentionally as part of the innate relationship between employees and employers. No president can undo this; we just have to live with it. It's not really right to be friends with the people who work for you. It's more empowering to acknowledge that a power differential exists than to ignore it. Employees feel the same way—they wouldn't want to tell you all their intimate life stories. You can be close, but you can't be friends.

As president of a large company, I felt I had to put a smile on my face in the morning even if I was concerned about the company. If I smiled, the company would smile. I had to be out there, thinking on my feet. If someone were to come to me with a question or problem, my natural tendency would be to take time to digest the information, go back to the person later, and say what I think. But as president, I was expected to have an immediate answer for everything. I also had to be somewhat more verbal than I might be normally. I enjoyed being a bit of an extrovert while I was doing it, but I noticed that when I got home, I didn't want to talk anymore. I wanted to balance my workday by doing physical activities that involved moving my hands. I wanted to change the energy and work on tasks that could be completed immediately, like ironing.

It can be difficult for a president to find people to talk to about what is really going on. I actually had only one woman within the company whom I could talk to. She was one of the first employees hired, and she had grown up with the company. I could talk openly to her because she knew everything that had happened since the company's inception. I also completed two executive education programs at Stanford University, and those gave me a certain amount of community in terms of learning that I wasn't alone in what I was dealing with. The first course was a two-week program for executives of smaller companies. The following year I took a marketing course. They were wonderful. There was a feeling of "Hey, we're in this boat, too. You're not that strange." We had some great professors, especially one business psychology professor who was a great morale booster. His advice helped me deal with whatever came up at Birkenstock.

For about eight years, I also belonged to a group of ten or so local business owners. That was my version of an advisory board. We met once a month. For the first half of the day a speaker would talk on a certain subject. During the second half of the day, we talked about our businesses. Each person had a few minutes to discuss what was going on. The business owners were very down to earth. If a person was going through a crisis, we would have a lot of discussion around that. But I noticed that even there, I filtered whatever I said. It would have been far more helpful if I had been with a group of fellow travelers who were also on the vision-driven business road. (I didn't know about Social Venture Network at that time.)

Except for these few outlets, I kept most everything in, and I balanced it with activities at home. Nobody really knew if we were going through hard times except the folks who wrote the checks. Then we started bringing in consultants to do team building and dialog training, and we began to implement ideas about open-book management. That was a really positive experience. Not everybody has that spirit of "Hey, this is my company, too, and I'm committed to it whether or not I get a bonus or a profit-sharing plan." But the training was definitely positive overall, and I continued it until I left.

During that time we had some not-so-good years, and I realized that it was healthier for me and my employees to have transparency in times of trouble. Whatever was happening would have been in the air anyway. Everyone would have known something was wrong, but no one would have known what, and that is scarier than handling the truth. There was a sense of relief in knowing that even though the situation could get pretty ugly, I was being honest and my employees knew where they stood. They had the choice to act accordingly. They knew I would continue to tell them the truth even if it was tough. That helped support morale. I still carried the whole burden of what was happening on my shoulders, but other people knew about it, and even if the burden and responsibility were mine, something shifted. I didn't have to worry about keeping secrets from people, I wasn't pulling the wool over anyone's eyes, and no PR lies were floating around to add a level of guilt. Overall, after the open-book management style was implemented, I felt more congruent, more honest, and more consistent.

Through all this, what always pulled me through was that I didn't focus on owning the company and being president; I focused on my passion for the product. During our ups and downs, I saw my job as being the missionary for it, and I would do everything necessary, everything possible, to make the product successful. By being a "servant" to the product, I grew into the "master" role, and I got used to having power. It felt natural. It was familiar and expected. How much this power originated from being the owner of the place became apparent to me only after I sold my company.

Three years after I sold the company, I was still chairman of the board. A conflict developed with our supplier in Germany, and I had a definite idea of how it should be handled. I advocated my point fervently. The rest of the board members were opposed to it. Finally, one member turned to me and said coldly, "Remember, you don't own this place anymore." There went my power—what a shock!

After I recovered, I realized she was right. I was no longer in charge. I had been president for a long time. Playing the role had been important for the success of the business, for the people connected to it, and, yes, even for myself. It had helped me tap into the strength and courage I had inside me. Still, when I was starting out, I had wished I could be "just me," and when this board member spoke to me the way she did, I realized I was allowed to bow out of the role. Or I thought I could. The truth is, this role-playing still continues years later. I have been built up into a legend. When people learn that I am the founder of Birkenstock USA, they ooh and aah about it. For the sake of the company, I still keep up appearances. It is amazing to me.

Staying Out of the Middle

■ **JOE, CREATIVE MACHINES**

I think a lot of stress occurs if the whole business is centered around the business owner. So, some of my decisions in the business are based on trying to get the pressure off me so I don't have to play the role of president all the time and make every single decision. For instance, I decided to hire Paula, our bookkeeper, because I didn't want everything centered around me. Or, at least on the surface, it wouldn't appear to be centered on me. Now that she is on board, she is the one who keeps records of employee vacations and time off. Even though I make all the decisions, she sets policy. It gives me some distance from that area because she is the mouthpiece.

When it comes to human resource decisions, including paid holidays, family leave, and so on, I would rather not make all the little decisions. This is both because I don't have the time and because I don't want to risk making arbitrary decisions based more on my personal preferences than on fair and rational thinking. The largest employer in Tucson is the University of Arizona, and all its policies are published online. In a state where laws are skewed in favor of the employer, the UA is relatively liberal and closer to my own values. Our policy has become "Whatever the UA does or nicer." An HR lawyer might tell me this policy is wrong, but it has worked for years. Now when employees ask me, "Are we going to take Martin Luther King Jr. Day off?" I don't have to get into a big political discussion that might be fraught with minefields.

Staying out of the middle is also one of the reasons we decided to do health care like we do it. With our size company, our insurance agent advised us not to do a group plan—every person should have an individual plan, and the company would reimburse the cost. Individual plans are quite good, and though group rates are good at first, as time goes on they rise, and once you've given up an individual plan to a group plan you can't go back. I also didn't want the stress of being in the middle of my employees' health problems. Now if they're having trouble with a claim, they talk to their insurance agent and not to me. If we had a group plan, I'd either have to get in the middle or I'd have to hire a human resources person to get in the middle because whenever you have a group "something," someone has to get in the middle—and in a small company, it's usually the owner.

Being the boss can be difficult. Not only do you have to make these kinds of decisions, but you also have to put on a brave public front and give the impression that there's a greater degree of order and purpose than there really is. Sometimes when we're late with our exhibits, when museums want to wait until the last minute to commit money or to commit to a particular job, when they want something unique and they want to control costs and they want to control the process and I think that getting the exhibits in on time is going to take a miracle, I just want to curl up in the corner and cry. But I can't. I have to put on a good face for my employees. It's part of a day's work. Playing roles is what we do in life all the time. But it's not the role that keeps me going; it's my employees. The fear of having to fire people or not being able to pay them is part of what makes me not want to throw in the towel during difficult times. If I quit, I would feel like I wasn't living up to a promise I made to them, which isn't entirely true. I should have the courage to fire people, but I don't want to have to.

Culturally, we have the need to succeed or, at least, the need not to fail. A while back I recognized that I felt as if I would be a personal failure if my business folded. A lot of people who have started businesses have a really personal relationship with their companies. Their sense of self is wrapped up in how well the business does. In some ways a business failure feels like a referendum on them. That's the more personal drive that makes people want to stay in the role of president. It might even be stronger than the company's mission.

I remember when I was able to work long hours, before I had a family. I was out running late at night and trying to make a certain decision that had to be made. Part of me just wanted to give up and say, "This is just too much pressure. I didn't want to get into this. I wanted to do this as a fun thing." The prospect of dissolving my own business and finding someplace nice and safe to work was appealing. The reasons piled up on both sides, and finally one little thing tipped the balance in favor of sticking with my own company: my father. I thought about how he had wanted to have his own company and didn't, partly because I came along. And I thought about what Jung said—how the unlived lives of our parents are what most deeply affects us—and I knew I had to see it through. I could have dropped out, quit playing president, and gotten another job with a museum like I had before I started my own company, but the thought of my father never having a chance to do what I was doing pushed me through. It was helpful to realize I was living a life that someone else only dreamed about, and it made the pressure of playing president worth it to me.

Weaving the Role with the Mission

■ MARIE, MS. FOUNDATION AND THE WHITE HOUSE PROJECT

When the Ms. Foundation started, I felt like I was acting on behalf of the women in this country, and I didn't worry about how I went about doing that. I found that when it came to getting funding, what mattered was not the content of what got funded or the value of it but what was known about it, what was out there. Perception was much more important than content when it came to money. I remember taking that in and realizing "You know, Marie, whether you like it or not, this is the world." I put on a good front so that people would fund the organization. Even if we were in the hole and we were not doing very well, I didn't let on because I knew image was very important. I didn't hear any ethical voice telling me I was doing wrong. I had very few times when I felt immoral about it. If I had said to people, "The Ms. Foundation is flat out of luck, broke, and dead," then they would have said, "Let it die," and the women of this country needed to think this was a big foundation. They needed hope and inspiration every day. So I knew I'd better get out there and do whatever I could to make it a big foundation. And I did.

I never felt like an imposter; I just felt like I was doing what I needed to do on behalf of our mission, and if this meant putting on a good front until we were strong, so be it. When I was growing up, I watched my working-class poor mother do the same. She knew how to present herself to the world in order to move up in social rank, to the middle class, so that her kids could have more in life and get more out of the world. She was able to get out of the strictures of her class by knowing how to dress. It didn't matter to her that this was a thin value for the world to judge her by. She wanted to get ahead, so she played by society's rules and dressed accordingly. I therefore understood that if you wanted to get to the next place, you had to look the part. Now I wear makeup and nice clothes because doing so reminds me that I can always make everything okay in the world if I think about how I present myself. Even after I became successful, my mother would remind me that dressing the part is important. After half of my relationship life, when I started to live with a woman, I called my mother—who came out of working-class, biblical values—and said, "I lived the first half of my life with men. I am going to live the second half of life with a woman. I found a woman I love." My mother asked me, "Does she know how to dress?" That was her response. She knew that how you present yourself can be a way to survive, and thrive, in the world.

I had a great mentor named Harvey Jenkins who taught me the same thing. He had a crew cut and looked pretty straight-laced, and he said to me, "Marie, you know the world doesn't really expect you to conform, not this country anyway. People just expect you to *look* like you are conforming." He was a radical man with radical ideas about the roots of change, and he was able to transcend societal norms and get things done because he didn't look like a rebel or a trouble starter.

The trouble with playing the role of a successful person who is representing a thriving organization is that you don't necessarily get rewarded for your work. Because I have to look a certain way and act sunny and positive in order to do my job, people think everything comes easily to me. One of my key advisers believed my work was effortless. She actually hated that things weren't more difficult. She would say, "Marie is so smart, she can just get money—it's so easy for her." There's a need for people to believe that you must be succeeding because you have good luck. God, I wish! There may be a few people in the world who are attractive and a lot comes to them, but most of us are just working every day. The truth is, I can be up at 4:30 a.m. and work until whatever time at night, and when I am out on the road people think I have a lot of energy, even if I am exhausted, because I put my game face on. The reason they think the work isn't difficult for me is that the organization was started by big names, and people think I already have a lot of resources. I don't want to be a martyr and say, "I work so hard," but I do want people to know the truth. When someone says your job is easy and doesn't take a lot of effort, it is like being seen inauthentically and not having your hard work acknowledged. It is important to be valued. The lie is letting each other believe that the job comes easily to some of us, which makes others say, "Why doesn't it come easily to me?" There's the opposite side of this, too. I've met many women of wealth who have to act like they don't have any money so they can be in the world. They come to board meetings wearing blue jeans. We all have to figure out how to present ourselves.

Because my presentation is so important in my work, I always have to make sure I haven't crossed the line into being only a persona. I have to ask myself, "Are you lying, or are you representing something you believe in?" The latter is a vision. Your product or organization should be your vision. I don't think I've ever told people something that I didn't truly believe, but if I feel like I am on the edge of doing that, I need to ask for help. I have to have people around me whom I can tell the truth to. I need to make sure I get moral, spiritual, and collegial support. If I have people I can confide in, I can feel whole every day. When we talk about our roles aloud, we remember that everyone is in some way dealing with her persona versus her core. There is no authentic self. We are integrating all parts of ourselves and figuring out which part we should show.

When the Authentic Self Is Troubled: To Share or Not to Share

■ **CAROL, PUTNEY PASTA**

I feel like I've grown into my role as president. It didn't come naturally, and I don't think it does for many people. As time went on, I became comfortable and confident with my role, yet the one thing that could be difficult was the feeling of transparency. I wanted to keep an open door, but it wasn't always appropriate to share everything with my employees.

As a socially responsible business owner, I felt like I had to protect my staff, and sometimes that meant not telling them the whole truth. For instance, my marriage fell apart during the time I owned the company. I hid that from the staff for a long time because my husband and I had started the business together. The story of our company was a couple's story: We had started with hot dogs and changed to pasta, and together we were Mr. and Mrs. Pasta. He had worked in the business for ten years. He stopped doing much in the last few years, and I made excuses for him. I think it was to protect him from whatever the staff might have felt about him. It's a small company, and everybody sees what everybody else does, so the staff knew my husband wasn't as active in the business as he had been. Plus, I wanted the staff to feel like the family was still together. They would ask me how Jon was doing, and I would say he had some health issues but that he was doing well, "Everything is fine." Until that point, we were an open-door company. It was part of our mission. I had always been very honest with my staff. But this time I felt it might be better to keep the issue private.

Another time I was not completely honest in my role as president was when the low-carb trend hit. It is difficult to be honest during stressful times. I had trouble keeping an open door. When manufacturing companies are in trouble, they try to keep the sales force going. They try to keep their employees' spirits up, hoping each month they can hang on, even if it's for only a few more months. In a values-driven company, it is important to tell the truth, but part of the problem with telling the truth is that if you are a supplier and word gets out that you are having trouble, the retailers might back out. They are at risk, too, and they want to make sure they can depend on you; if not, they need to look for a different supplier. If they feel like you are a sinking ship, chances are you *are* a sinking ship. On a personal level, it is important to protect your pride and dignity. When a situation changes, you might not feel you can share it publicly so you internalize it.

When things are going badly and you are president, you also wonder if people can separate you from your company. Even if your company is failing, it doesn't mean you are a failure, but it's difficult to know whether other people realize that. I remember being at a board meeting for a local independent food store that was in deep financial trouble. I could relate to what was going on, and as I was making suggestions for some really tough decisions, I couldn't help thinking, "If people knew how badly my business is doing, would they still think that I knew what I was doing? If my business fails, how can I give them guidance for their business?" In reality, because of my own problems, I could better see what other troubled businesses were going through, but if they knew what was happening with me, I wondered if they would trust me.

I've been in the community for thirty years, and because I owned a business, it might have looked like I was successful and had a lot of money. It didn't matter what the business was doing; that's the perception. After a while, I felt like I was in a play, and I had to continue in the role of a successful businessperson. We all adapt to that role in different ways.

Approaching Burnout

■ TOM, NORTHEAST DELTA DENTAL

Playing president is a lot of pressure, and about two and a half years ago I realized I was headed toward total burnout. One day I looked at my life and realized, "Oh, my God, I am going to be a disaster if I don't get some help." I felt like I was in my own movie, racing from one meeting to the next, feeling that if I missed anything I would crash and burn. I was not really enjoying anything. Life had become a series of checking items off my list. I'd go to my son's soccer game, then I'd go straight to a Red Cross board meeting, and then I'd head back to the office for a teleconference. I was running myself ragged, and I was also trying to be a mentor for people internally. I was hurting my employees and my family because I had very little energy left for them. All my systems were maxed out. My life had become the ultimate rat race. No one would have known it because I didn't suddenly stop showing up; I still made it to every meeting and event. But I was dragging myself home at midnight, totally exhausted, and then I would have the minimum amount of sleep and wake up at 5:00 a.m. to do it all over again.

When I realized I was headed for burnout, I hired a team of resource people. I had gained somewhere between fifteen and thirty pounds, so first I hired a personal trainer. I also hired a presentation consultant. Because I am an introvert, giving speeches was really stressful, and I needed help in that department. Then I found a massage therapist. I hired a family coach because we had four teenagers, including twin boys, and we needed some guidance. Basically, I hired eight or nine people. They were speaking from the level of spirit and soul. These folks all had really beautiful wisdom. They asked me some deep questions about the meaning of my day-to-day life. They helped me take an honest look at my life to see what was really going on. And they all told me the same thing: I had to trim back in order to be healthy.

The whole process of getting healthy again was a year-long struggle. I was on so many boards and also trying to run my company (which is actually four companies and four different boards), so I was spending a tremendous amount of time at night and in the morning at board meetings. My presentation consultant had the great idea of using my calendar as a landscape. She looked at it and said, "Is this how you want the landscape of your life to look?" We looked at which boards I could drop off of as my term limits came up. It's very difficult for me to say no. I always want to say yes to any reasonable or unreasonable request that an organization offers me. It felt good in the short term to say yes, but it was hurting me in the long run. So my consultant encouraged me to say yes only to customer requests to speak about oral health or to something I was passionate about, like 5K road races or the Red Sox. With those parameters I was able to start saying no, and I trimmed back on quite a few external commitments. It hurt internally at first, but I've gotten better at realizing I am saying no for the right reasons. Saying no also means taking time out for myself. When I get a massage, I drive out to Keene, where my cell phone doesn't work, so even on the way there, I can decompress. During the ninety-minute session, I don't have to talk; I can just sleep or relax. That has helped me tremendously to rejuvenate.

Before I got to a place of burnout, my resources for dealing with my company were more traditional. I was involved with a network of CEOs, and if I had a business problem, I could discuss it with them. They weren't my bosses or my subordinates, so I could talk openly about business issues. They might be running companies in completely different industries, so they were able to give fresh insights on the nuts and bolts of business plans and expertise on issues like technical and personnel problems. But this was a somewhat superficial outlet because the CEOs focused only on business. I didn't feel comfortable saying, "Hey, guys, I'm about to become a basket case." I am still involved with them, but they aren't nearly as helpful as my more spiritual advisers. In terms of where I am going personally and where I think the success of the company is, it lies with this new group, this new team I'm involved with.

I used to joke that I had gone from being a totally low-maintenance person to being a person who needs nine people to help me through life. Then the suggestion was made that I shouldn't talk about accessing resources in such a self-deprecating way. If I am setting an example and trying to get others to know it is okay to get help, I shouldn't use self-deprecating language because people might not know if I am joking or not. One of the things I'm doing a better job of now is explaining to my employees that it's okay to ask for help. I'm very free about telling people I use a presentation consultant. I've offered her services to a number of our employees who make speeches. People know it's okay to step away from the office for an hour or so to let off some steam. I try to demonstrate that myself. Now we have a beautiful fitness center next door with a trainer available, and several running groups run during the day. I am trying to get the message across about the importance of asking for help, setting boundaries, taking time out, and caring for ourselves. And I am trying to do it without attaching a stigma to it.

What We Learned

In these stories, our values-driven entrepreneurs described the challenges of juggling a lot of balls while playing their roles as president. They had to tell the truth, stay true to their missions, project success to the outside world, keep smiles on their faces, and try to take care of their stress levels at the same time—not any easy task! We can learn from each other how to keep all those balls in the air. It starts with acknowledging your own story about playing the role of president. Which aspects are easy, and where is it more difficult? Can you see yourself and your role clearly? And where can you get the help you need? Here are some ideas:

- *Try not to compare your insides with everyone else's outsides.* Remember that no matter how someone looks, he is probably working just as hard as you are and feeling just as scared and anxiety ridden. Focus on your own truth rather than imagining someone else's.

- *Reach out to another entrepreneur and tell her the truth.* Internalizing stress just makes it bigger. If you can find someone to talk to and be yourself with, you might be able to alleviate some of the stress that arises from trying to keep a smile on your face and acting like everything is great.

- *Do something physical.* A lot of CEOs do something at the end of the day to check out, like drink a glass of wine or something stronger, but this doesn't necessarily take care of the body. You can try tai chi, running, tennis, yoga, or workouts at a gym. Put these activities on your calendar. If you schedule time to take care of yourself, your employees might be more apt to follow suit.

- *Enroll in an executive education program for CEOs.* It can be almost impossible to find someone in your family or your workplace who understands the pressures of playing president. When you join an executive education program, not only will you see that other CEOs are going through some of the same issues that you are, but you can also gain skills and tools for dealing with some of the major problems that arise when you are president. You might also find mentors that can help you.

- *Recognize the signs of approaching burnout and get the help you need.* Get a massage, hire a coach, make a therapy appointment, find a personal trainer, or take an art class! Somehow you have to find something that fits into your day. This may seem counterintuitive, but by taking the time, you actually make the time. You will sleep better and work more effectively, and your people will be happier because you are happier. Start with your own mental health, and then you will be on the road to having a healthy company. You must have this conviction to get help or it won't carry to your employees. If you can learn to take care of you, your business will be positively affected.

- *Form that advisory board early and use it often.*

These suggestions have been gleaned from stories we heard from our entrepreneurs. Use the ones that work for who you are, and leave the rest for another day or pass them on to a fellow CEO who might be finding it difficult to integrate his own role as president with who he is in his core.

■ **PRACTICAL TIP**

Part A: Find a Way to Make Yourself Take the First Step.
Take your head out of the sand or pick yourself up off the floor, dust yourself off, and take just one step forward. If you can find a way to take that first step, you'll find that the next ones are easier.

Part B: Know When Not Acting Is the Correct Action.
A lot of problems can be solved by taking the counterintuitive step of *not* making a decision when things are most stressful, customers are screaming, and your key staff is pushing hard

for something to happen. This is not a recommendation for putting your head in the sand and not dealing with issues—it's just that sometimes a delay will allow the problem to shift, give you time to get more information, or let everyone calm down until a simple solution can be seen.

■ PRACTICAL TIP
Do Something Tangible
As our companies grow many entrepreneurs find their work becomes less and less tangible. It can help to garden or paint or build something or clear brush—something physical that you can point to to say, "I did *that* today."

■ PRACTICAL TIP
Volunteer for a Local Nonprofit
Find a cause you care about that is completely different from your everyday work and volunteer for an hour. Try something you have never done before: serve food at a homeless shelter, stuff envelopes for a year-end fund-raising drive, bake cookies for a school bake sale, or do whatever sounds different and useful. Remember, though, do this in balance. Don't overdo it and don't overcommit your time.

9

Moving on

There comes a unique stage in our relationships with our companies when it is time to leave. We will all move on from our companies at some point for various reasons: we hit retirement age, our business fails, we burn out, or we see that it's a logical time to harvest some (or all) of the value we have built. We have heard stories of entrepreneurs who have decided, for all different reasons, to make a change and move on. There are a lot of ways to exit. We can merge with another company, go public, sell to our employees, find a financial buyer, or just pay off the bills and close the doors. But how do we know for ourselves when it's time to leave? What is important to consider when thinking about a new ownership structure? How can we ensure that our values of social responsibility carry on? What if our business is failing and we need to shut down?

In this chapter, Lisa describes her values-driven focus on finding the right equity partner. Margot tells us about the challenges of selling her business to her employees. Carol tells us the truth about what happened when her company was on the brink of closing. And Gary gives us great advice about asking better questions and remembering that nothing is impossible.

Exiting with the Values in Place

■ **LISA**

One of the greatest pieces of advice I got from my advisory board was offered by John Leehman. He told me that the best way to run your company is to position it to be sold in three years. At the end of that time you can either sell it or emotionally "buy" it. I went through this process at the same time as Tami Simon from Sounds True Recording. At the end of the three years, I sold my company and she "bought" hers.

When I turned forty, I started to position my company to be sold. A myriad of circumstances were converging to confirm that it was time for me to leave. My customer base had consolidated into much bigger companies, and it was difficult to remain a regional supplier—we would need to be national or at least multiregional. My vendors and ingredient suppliers had also become larger as more and more big companies bought out the small guys and made an entry into organic products. My personal relationships with both customers and suppliers were disappearing as their organizations became more corporate. My company needed to be significantly larger, yet I had absolutely no interest in running a $200 million company. I also faced the reality that this business was not really my passion, and I was becoming more burned out, stressed, and unpleasant to be around.

I had to face that the time had come to leave, and I had to begin to let go of my positional power. I had been in this business since I was twenty-one years old, and my identity was very wrapped up in it. I wrestled with a lot of conflicting emotions as I was making my decision. My company was the largest woman-owned business in the state and one of the top ten fastest growing companies. I enjoyed being involved with local and state issues and having my opinion sought out.

I also had to start thinking about money differently. In a growing manufacturing company, anytime I had money I poured it back into the business. Have some money? Upgrade computers. Have some more money? Increase inventory. Borrowed some money? Replace aging equipment. But as I started to position the company to be sold, I had to place the focus back on myself and ask the question "How much is enough?" To support my family, cover health-care costs, give money away, and invest in new ventures, how much do I need?

I also needed to figure out how to exit the company so that it kept the same values of social responsibility that were embedded in my business every day. I couldn't just abandon these principles on the way out the door. I made a list of all the values that would need to remain present to be sure I found the right buyer. When I first wrote the list, it was pages and pages long, but I kept refining and distilling it until I had four bedrock values.

My first value was a commitment to keep the jobs in southern Vermont. The jobs needed to continue to offer livable wages with good benefits. One of the core values of Vermont Bread Company had always been to provide livable jobs to the "bottom third" of our school system. These jobs allow people to care for themselves and their families in a workplace where the key value is respect.

The second value was that the buyer had to have a history of granting stock to employees. At my company, I often said we were running on "bootstrap and bank debt." I was fortunate to have bankers that believed in me and that let me operate two years ahead of my balance sheet. I actually never knew what it was like to have a positive number in the checkbook because I lived in my line of credit. At one time my debt-to-worth ratio was 11:1. It was important to me to couple the new incoming equity investment with ownership for our key employees.

The third value was that the new owners had to maintain a commitment to certified organic production. Under my leadership, most of our new products for the past few years were certified organic, and this dedication to sustainable agriculture was critical to me.

The fourth value was that the new owners had to have enough money to realize the vision. I had met too many people with what I refer to as the "Wimpy strategy." Remember Wimpy from the Popeye cartoons? "I'll gladly pay you on Tuesday for a hamburger today." We had already run this company without adequate cash, and that was one stress I wanted to take off my employees when I exited.

With those four values in mind, I was fortunate to work with a wonderful man, Steve Mintz, who found a buyer (actually a few buyers) who met all my criteria. Still, it's always hard to know if you've made the right decision. A few months after I sold a majority interest of Vermont Bread Company, I led a tour through the plant. Many of my employees came up to me and said they were sad not to be working with me anymore. The opposite was also true, though—they thanked me for providing new opportunities for them in a much larger company. One brave woman pointed out that she appreciated how rested I looked; she had been worried to see me so burned out at the end.

Since I sold my company, I feel like I get younger and my energy lightens every day. I've joked that I would never, ever be an employer or an employee again. But who knows? I serve on boards, I am still employed by the private equity company that invested in Vermont Bread Company so that I can help with acquisitions, and I am writing this book. That seems to be keeping me out of trouble for now. As I "fade to black," it feels, at least at this point in time, like it's going as well as I could have imagined in my wildest dreams.

Handing It Over to the Employees

■ **MARGOT**

In 1991 I began to ponder how my company could go on, how this complicated thing that had grown up over the years could survive without me. I had become a figurehead of the enterprise, and in order for me to move on, this had to change. The logical step for most entrepreneurs is to find a competitor that will buy the company. Several parties were interested, and I could have made a lot of money that way if a deal had worked out. But they weren't really interested in the company as an ongoing enterprise; they were mostly interested in the brand name, which had become almost a household word. A well-known brand is a very valuable asset. As a brand extension, it can be put on all kinds of merchandise and can be very profitable. But we did not own the name—we only had the rights to use it in this country—so we couldn't sell it. And I didn't want to dilute the brand by putting it on unrelated goods. After all, it was a manufacturing brand, not just a marketing brand.

I asked Mr. Birkenstock whether he wanted to buy all or part of our company. He and his family discussed it and couldn't come to an agreement. Finally, they told me that it wasn't in their plan to own any foreign distributors. They wanted them to remain separate entities. At that point I decided to hand over the company to the employees. We already had an ESOP (employee stock ownership plan) in place. We had a generous profit-sharing plan and had always funded it in cash. One year when no cash was available, I paid the plan with stock. It diluted my own interest, but my employees had helped me build the company, so I wanted them to share in the profits with me. By the time I was thinking of stepping out, the employees owned about 10 percent of the company, and I began to plan for them to acquire the company over time. I felt that would be the best answer—after all, as employees, they should be very much invested in the company's future success. That next year I sold another 30 percent to the employees on a note with the promise of selling all when the first portion was paid off. The first portion was paid off about five years later. What happened after that is a long tale. I retired and gave up active leadership but stayed on as board chair. Things did not go as well as anticipated, and I had to learn once again that the best laid plans can fall apart. It is the nature of life.

People ask me why the employees didn't do better as the company owners. The answer is not simple. Several events happened at the same time. First, Mr. Birkenstock retired the same year I did and handed the reins over to his three sons. The leadership change on both sides of the ocean put a real strain on relationships. The sons had created five different brands on the "footprint" of the Birkenstock design principle. When I was CEO, I had tried to market all five brands under the umbrella of the mother brand. When the sons took over, they started their own distribution companies in the United States for each of the brands, and this created a big problem for our new leadership, eventually eroding the relationship between Mr. Birkenstock's sons and the employee-owned company here.

Another reason the employees struggled is that there is a big difference between having all the employees own the company versus having one owner in charge. While I was head of Birkenstock USA, I felt we developed a good ownership culture in our company. We had financial training for everyone, team-building sessions, and problem-solving forums. In theory, the employees should have felt the same ownership as I did, but when they actually owned the company, there wasn't just one signature on the line of credit—one person wasn't making promises to the bank that she had to uphold. It wasn't as though one person's house was on the line, making her respond quickly and effectively. Employees often don't feel a personal connection to the fate of a company, and they wind up running it like any corporation.

Another thing that happened after I left was that the bank, which had been easy on credit, suddenly tightened the reins. At the same time, pressure from Germany to buy more led to inventory purchases that were too large. Cash became scarce. Bills couldn't get paid on time. When the company couldn't pay the bills, trust with the Germans eroded, much-needed sandal shipments were held up, and a chain reaction was set in motion that spelled trouble for everybody.

Three years after I sold the company, the situation had not improved. The employees were having a lot of trouble. The youngest Birkenstock brother wanted to help. He was interested in the U.S. business and asked to buy a majority portion. Writing contracts back and forth took forever. When one side thought there was an agreement and all that was needed was a signature, the other side would say no, and someone would be very angry, so the deal would fall through. I saw that the company was going in the wrong direction, but I could do nothing to rescue it. It is very difficult to see your child "drown." I was at a loss, and I felt that I had done the best I could. At that point I resigned totally, board and all. It was difficult—letting go is a grieving process, and it takes time to recover. It took me over a year before I could sit back and just watch what was happening with curiosity and objectivity.

The German company did finally buy the U.S. company. It was a new beginning. The ESOP is gone, but a more secure future is ahead. How do I feel about an ESOP? I still think it is an excellent vehicle to engage people in running a business because it helps them to look further into the future as opposed to focusing only on the immediate bottom line. It's not easy having an ESOP, though. An ownership culture needs to be nurtured, which may be easier in a smaller company. Still, in the final analysis, it is not the size of the company but the commitment of the management team that makes it work.

Will I ever totally break free from Birkenstock? In all those years with the company, I had become "Mrs. Birkenstock" to the world and will probably always be remembered that way. Just a few weeks ago I was in San Diego, and I visited a Birkenstock specialty store near my hotel. I met a woman there who was trying on sandals. When she learned who I was, she practically screamed, "Thank you. You saved my life! I could never do without these shoes." She went on to buy three pairs. Experiences like this make everything worthwhile. They warm my heart and make me feel like a success after all.

Would I do it again? You bet. I know so much more now, it would be easier sailing. The most important advice I have for you is this: It is lonely at the top. Stay open and keep learning. Get all the help you can. The final decisions will still all be yours, but a good advisory board is a mighty helper!

Getting Through the Last Stage (Laughter, a Gym, a Pond, and a Fling)

■ **CAROL, PUTNEY PASTA**

The end of my company began when we lost a big account we were dependent on and we had just burned through all our cash because of the low-carb craze. We had a couple of new prospects, but they didn't last. I was dependent on make-or-break deals with two customers. I figured if we could get just one, maybe we could survive a little longer. It was a juggling act. I felt like I was getting bombarded everywhere. I really couldn't find any more places to cut back. You can usually cut another few percent somewhere, but I felt like we were as trim as we could be. We didn't have a big production staff to begin with. Only seven people were left, but they were a dream staff. If we cut back and then we got more business, we would have had to max out those few remaining people and eventually would have lost them because they would have burned out. Plus, if both of the accounts came in, I would have enough money to hire back the people we let go, and then they might not be available anymore. In the end, everyone stayed.

My employees showed up every day, and I showed up, too, because I felt that if I stayed home, I would be giving in to the fact that I was losing the battle. I have a very strong sense of responsibility to the business. My employees kept saying, "Are we going to make it? It's not looking good." A number of them came to me and said, "I'm here until the doors close, Carol." They were great people. Even though I tried to put a positive spin on our situation, they knew what was going on. Still, I wanted them to know I wouldn't quit easily. I wasn't going down without a fight. So I kept the doors open. By showing up, I kept some hope alive that we could make something happen.

I'd arrive with a smile on my face because my being there provided a sense of comfort to the employees, but I could smile only long enough to get through the door of my office. Then I shut the door. I used to always have an open-door policy, but during that time, I never had my door open. I didn't want to hear about the daily issues. The little idiosyncrasies that I would have overlooked before were magnified. I can't tell you how many times I thought it would be easier to shut the doors for good and stop the pain, but I didn't want to disappoint my two support team members, Lisa Lorimer and Steve Mintz. In my heart I didn't think there was any way I could win the battle. It hurt so much. I wanted to be taken out of the misery of losing this company that I had worked twenty-two years to build. I just thought, "Kill me quickly." It felt like a slow torture, like I was reading a book, and I wanted to go to the last page to see how the book ends. It looked like we were never going to get to the end. It was really hard to accept.

Once I came to terms with the fact that my company was not going to make it to the end of the year, all desire to stay connected started to diminish. I lost humor and kindness. I was sad, and that's not me, I'm not a sad person, but I kept thinking, "Oh my gosh, twenty-two years, and I'm going to have to kiss it good-bye. Life isn't fair." I felt like I couldn't fight to keep it going because no matter how much I fought for it, nothing would make a difference. I hit a wall. I didn't want to be with anybody. I didn't want to see anyone. I still went to work, but some days I'd come home, get on the couch, cover myself with a blanket, and just lie there. I wouldn't put on music or news or anything. This lasted three or four months, through one whole winter. I felt if I got a good night's sleep, which was rare, I would be okay. So I would take a sleeping pill, unplug the phone, and get into bed at eight o'clock. The next day I might wake up feeling much better, and I'd start the morning off great, ready to rally again. Then I would get to work and all the vendors would call and scream, the bank would pressure me, and my assistant would take the calls and say, "All I can do is take a message, and we'll look into it and make sure it's in payables." I was dodging everyone. I don't usually dodge issues because I know they don't go away, but I just didn't have the strength for it. By the end of the day I was ready to go back to bed and cocoon under my blanket.

At that point, I knew the stress was going to a new level, and that wasn't healthy. I wasn't doing anything with love—everything was just another responsibility. It was an overwhelming feeling. I was impatient with everyone: gas-station attendants, store clerks, whomever. I have an elderly mother, and I even lost my patience with her. I also have an amazing son. I have never had a fight with him in my whole life. He's been very easy, and we've always had a really good relationship. He was the only one I enjoyed sharing time with. He knew everything that was going on. He was twenty-five years old and in sales for the company. I would call him and ask him to come down from Burlington when I needed his company. I could be open and honest with him, and he was very supportive. He would come home and say, "Okay, Mom, where's my list? You got things you want me to do for you? Here, I'll go stack some wood." One day I realized I couldn't share quite so much with him because he would have a hard time staying motivated in sales if I said, "What's the point? We're going to be out of business anyway." I needed him to stay focused and motivated on the off chance that we did pull out of this, so I had to stop sharing with him. I had to try to put on a facade even for him. Sometimes I snapped at him. I didn't like what I was turning into.

I had a wonderful network of friends, but they weren't able to do much in terms of giving sound advice on the business side. I was telling everyone, "I'm not going to make it." And everyone was saying, "You're going to make it." And I would say, "You don't understand how bad it is this time. I'm not going to make it." And they would say, "Oh, yes you are." They thought they were supporting me.

Up to that point, my life had been pretty easy. I felt charmed. I'd never had major hurdles to overcome. I came from a good family. We were comfortable. I could go to whatever school I wanted to attend. Life was never hard. I always thought some guardian angel was looking out for me, telling me I was lucky. Whenever I got close to an edge, I would get pulled back. My lawyer and my bankruptcy attorney were always saying, "You are just so lucky, I don't believe it. You've called me so many times to tell me you were almost out of business, and then it always turns out okay in the end." They were right. I felt like that so many times, but this was the first time I was saying to my guardian angel, "Alright, what's the plan here? How come this isn't working out? What are you waiting for? Am I going to have a heart attack before you pull me out of this one?"

We were pursuing one potential buyer. It was a long shot, but I kept at it. The buyer finally made an offer to the bank to buy everything. It was a great offer, but in the end the deal fell through because I found out that my main competitor in natural foods had just been purchased by the largest distributor in the industry and I had to disclose that. Still, that news gave me hope because if my competitor could sell its company in this environment, then I probably could, too.

That hope was there, but what really got me through were a couple of good friends, a gym, a fling, and a pond. My two friends Lisa and Steve were the only people who didn't feel like a risk to talk to. They were both business owners and understood the issues inherent in running a business. Lisa and I had a long history of being there for each other. We sat on each other's advisory boards. We didn't judge each other, and there wasn't a sense of superiority about whose business was bigger, or who was the expert. We had a tremendous amount of regard for one another. We sort of flip-flopped on who had the issues and who was supporting whom at certain times. It wasn't as if we were best friends outside of work, but the trust between us was deeper than in any of my other friendships. We were both in manufacturing, which has its own issues that are different from those of sales and marketing. So we connected at a peer level, which is a beautiful thing. When I told her something, I knew it wouldn't go any further. Every day during this time, she and Steve would call me and make it their goal to get me to laugh at least once during the conversation. It was really healing for me to access that ability to go deep and find the laughter that was always there. No matter how dark it got, somehow that muscle or that spirit that was connected to laughter and resilience was still alive.

I had gained about thirty pounds during that time, and with Steve and Lisa's encouragement, I hired a personal trainer and made myself go to the gym three days a week. I was committed because I had this trainer, and I never wanted to let her down. I had to have someone like her to hold me accountable or I would get off the highway in Putney and turn right and be home in ten minutes. If I went left I'd be at the gym in the same amount of time, and I would be there for an hour to an hour and a half, so it was really tempting to go right and go home. More often than not, when I didn't have an appointment with Carla, I'd get to that crossroads and I'd go right because I felt like I needed to be home to be by myself. Being alone was my first choice, but the gym was much healthier and made me feel better in the end.

Another thing that helped was my winter fling. He was the first person I'd been with in thirty years besides my two husbands. I called him a transitional guy. That romance came at a perfect time. I still didn't leave the house, but this fling lit my heart and brought some sparkle back. I'd been heavyhearted for a long time, and this helped hold the old car battery charge for a while. It made everything not as scary and more manageable. Before the fling, my life had been one dimensional. It was just work and sadness and fear. This was the only thing that could take my mind totally away. I didn't think about the business for hours.

Then I also discovered the pond. The pond was sort of a metaphor for everything that was happening during that time. In the summer, I have to mow my lawn and my fields. I mow my fields with my tractor and my two acres of lawn with my riding mower. I have a reputation for mowing—that I will risk my life and limb for another two inches of lawn. One day, I was mowing down by the pond on my property. I'd been alone for this horrible autumn, winter, and spring, and that summer day I was thinking how gorgeous the place looked, yet I wasn't really enjoying it. I hadn't put the flowers on the deck; I hadn't planted a garden because it felt too time-consuming. I had to be really careful what I did with my time because I had only two days a week at home, and there was always stuff to be done. It was a hot day, and I hadn't been swimming all summer. I started to think how I had this pond as a resource but never used it because I always heard my mother's voice in my head telling me never to swim by myself. That day I thought, "Forget it. If I drown, I drown—it will put me out of my misery. This pond is here, and I am going swimming." I took off all my clothes and jumped in. I swam around for a bit and then I thought, "How am I going to get out of this pond?" The ladder didn't work, but I managed to get up onto the dock, thinking, "Thank God no one is around." But that day was my liberation. I realized that I had choices, and I get to make them. I had chosen to isolate myself and mourn. This first venture into the pond was a different kind of choice. The pond saved my life. When things were awful, every sunny weekend day I would go down there and go skinny-dipping, floating around on a raft for hours by myself, and that was the most calming, relaxing thing I did all week long. There is something about water.

What new entrepreneurs need to remember is that you will eventually recover and continue living. Life goes on. You will figure it out. One day after a good night's sleep, when I'd had a few days respite from all the bombardments, I showed up at work, picked up the phone, and called every one of the vendors who had been calling and calling. Then I called the bank.

I knew it was the right thing to do. I had wanted to do it before, but I hadn't had the strength. I could do it now because I'd refueled—I'd gotten a little break and caught my breath. I had the strength to face what I needed to face. The people who had been calling were people I had done business with for a long time. Out of respect for them and for my own feeling of doing the right thing, I finally began dealing with it. I didn't think I could possibly do it at that point, but I did.

I believed if the business closed, that would be one more public humiliation, but I didn't have to face any humiliation because the business sold at the end. What a difference it makes to be able to say, "I sold my company." Even if I got almost nothing for it, that was so much better than having to say, "We had to close the doors." I don't know for sure because I didn't have to close my doors, but I think the difference in how it could have ended and how I would have felt are like night and day.

I feel like my knowledge is there and it's being appreciated by the new owners. I don't know if I would have gotten that same respect or if I would have felt that same confidence going in and helping a pasta company if I'd had to close the doors. I know a guy who's running a pasta plant, and he's already said, "Maybe one day you'll come in and run my plant." No, I won't. I'd be happy to help him out, but I don't want to go back to running a plant. Because I sold the company, there's that respect, though. He can actually appreciate all that I know. Would he feel the same way if I said to him, "I'm looking for a job running a plant—I just had to close mine down"? I don't know. It is all the same experience, all the same knowledge, all the same everything—except how the world perceives you. If you sell your company, whether it's for a dollar or for ten million, to the public it's all the same.

Now I've lost thirty pounds. I feel like I felt when I was twenty years old: emotionally lighter, lighthearted, free, happy, and upbeat.

Why Not?

■ GARY, STONYFIELD FARM

When I decided to try to get my shareholders an exit, I wanted to do it right. Stonyfield was my baby. It was my whole life. It was, at that time, eighteen years of work. I looked at the conventional choices that were available. One choice was to sell the company. I didn't want to do that because I didn't want to stop running it. I just wanted to get the shareholders their much-deserved liquidity. Another choice was to take the company public. After watching the experience of Ben & Jerry's, I knew that taking it public was basically selling the company no matter how you sweet-talk and lather it on. I also looked at a DPO (direct public offering), but when I sat on the board of Blue Fish, another company that had been through that, I saw what a disaster it was. It was just a modified version of taking the company public. In the end, though, I had to learn the hard way—through my own process.

At first, I thought we would take the business public, and I put together a special board committee. We spent a year interviewing bankers. Eventually, we narrowed our choices down to two bankers. We spent about $100,000 or more during the process. The night before the special board committee was supposed to make the decision, I realized I didn't want to do it, and I pulled out.

Our next choice was to start all over again by finding a banker who would help us create a joint venture. That was very different from our last search. The two bankers we had chosen would have been good if we had wanted to take the company public, but they were not right for a joint venture. We ended up picking a very different banker. I ultimately hired this particular one because when I told him what I wanted done and asked him, "Do you think I can do it?" he said, "I don't know, but I'm willing to try." That's all I wanted to hear. After I chose the banker, I spent a year talking to prospects. The first person I sat down with was the head of M&A (mergers and acquisitions) at a large international food corporation. She was the first of many, many people from many different companies I would talk to. I told her what I wanted to do, and she literally laughed at me. She took her glasses off, set them in front of her, and said in her very heavy French accent, "That's hilarious, Gary. You mean to tell me you want to sell me 80 percent of your company and still remain in control?" I said yes and she laughed again. She thought that was very funny.

The slogan "Nothing is impossible" is true—because I wound up achieving exactly what I set out to do when I closed the deal two years later. After a year of looking, we found two companies willing to do this deal. Most of the time I knew within ten to fifteen seconds of meeting the person sitting down in front of me that it wasn't going to happen. Finally, we began negotiating seriously with these two companies. It took about two more years. The head of M&A was already gone by then. I called her up and said, "I just want you to know it really did happen." She laughed again.

There's knowing when to fold, but there's also knowing when not to fold, knowing when to persist in finding success when all the doors seem to be leading to failure. I didn't start with a solution. My process wasn't linear; I learned while I went through it. I just kept asking better questions. That's what got us to a better answer. I used my Hampshire College background. I always describe Hampshire as the perfect business school for entrepreneurs because you design your own curriculum, you don't get grades or credits, and there are no requirements. You progress through a series of evaluations called modes of inquiry where your faculty members kick you into asking questions. They are constantly saying, "Have you asked this? Have you asked that? Have you thought of that?" The final product—the thesis or the business plan—is not the measure of success; the process of creating the plan is what's important. I have three kids, and I tell them all the time that what they are learning today in school is going to be outdated before they blink. What I learned in my math and science classes as a kid is a tenth of what is out there today. We learned maps in geography that are completely obsolete now. But it doesn't matter because gaining the information is not what's important. To know is not enough. The goal of the learning process needs to be to gain the confidence that you can learn anything under any circumstances.

Now I counsel entrepreneurs who are facing that question: To sell or to close their doors? The fact is, there's a different question out there: Why not? On the boards I sit on, those are my two favorite words. When someone says, "You can't do this," I say, "Why not?" And we inevitably come up with something. It's not always a better solution, but you certainly get a different solution if you stick with that question.

What We Learned

When it is time to exit a values-based company, bringing our values to the forefront can help us make an exit that is in alignment with our original mission. Our entrepreneurs' stories highlight a few ideas that helped them during this process:

- *Position your company to be sold in three years.* At the end of the three-year period, either "buy" the company emotionally and recommit to it or begin the process of selling it.

- *Answer the question, "How much is enough?"* How much will it take to pay off your debts, take care of your employees, support your family, cover health-care costs, do your philanthropy, and invest in new ventures? Write down the numbers and add them up.

- *Make a list of your core values that will lead you through the process.* Start with a long list, everything you can think of. Then go through the list and find the bedrock values.

- *Identify the correct type of buyer for your company.* Ask yourself if the right buyer is your employees, a competitor, a complementary company, a financial buyer, or a public offering. Try to find other companies that have sold in various ways and compare their processes.

- *Get a good team around you.* The team may include members of your advisory board or not. Find the right people to give you the support you need. Whom you choose for the team will depend on your core values and whom you are targeting as a buyer.

- *Find a way to take care of yourself during this time.* Float in a pond, laugh every day, go to a gym, sing, or do something else!

- *Keep asking better questions throughout the process.* Remember to keep asking, "Why not?"

■ **PRACTICAL TIP**

Laugh and Laugh and Then Laugh Again

Carol tells the story of talking to two colleagues every day when her business was the most troubled. They had a pact that every day during their phone calls together, they must belly laugh at least three times. It helps a lot.

■ **PRACTICAL TIP**

Float in Water

Any water will do—hot tub, pool, pond, ocean, bathtub.

Conclusion

Tell *your* story

At a Social Venture Institute one year, a young entrepreneur was providing a case study about the challenges of her company. In a thoughtful and thorough presentation, she told us how just a few years ago she started Knotty Boy Dread Stuff, a company that distributes products to take care of dreadlocks. Knotty Boy Dread Stuff was going through some of the same trials and tribulations that we address in this book. As the respondents were getting ready to give their feedback, we could see how nervous the entrepreneur had become. The first words Lisa said to her were, "You are doing everything right, and given where your business is, these are all the *right* problems to have." The woman gave a very visible sigh of relief. Later, at this same conference, Lisa saw something that has always stuck with her: Margot Fraser and this same young woman were sitting at a picnic table with their heads together. Margot was following up on her case study and talking intently to her about her financial statements. That's how this book began.

As seasoned business entrepreneurs, we can't go back in time and tell our younger selves that these are good problems to have, every leap looks like the biggest leap until the next one comes along, we all screw up, every business owner is playing a role, learning to trust yourself goes back to your core values, Goliaths' shadows are big until you build the multi-legged stool, owning your numbers is usually more effective than burying your head in the sand, creating an advisory board can save your company, and you can still think of yourself as a success even if you have to close your doors. We can't offer our younger selves practical tips and self-care strategies so that we won't take the road to burnout. But we *can* tell the truth to other entrepreneurs. We can share our stories and perhaps help others who are trying to make a living while also making a better world. And so we wrote this book.

The intent of this book is not to address all the tough stuff we have ever had to face while running values-based businesses. We could have written much, much more about legal battles, difficult employees, the economy, federal agencies, natural disasters, and on and on. Our goal was simple: to offer stories, ideas, and tips that reflect the truth about creating healthy ecosystems within our companies. On these pages, we tried to acknowledge the balancing act inherent in staying integrated with our core values: respect for one another and ourselves; a profitable, sustainable company with positive cash flow; livable wages to stakeholders; and a low impact on the environment. Using business as a tool to positively impact our world is a radical act, and it isn't always easy. Sometimes when we are wrestling with the tough stuff, it can be hard to find stories that reflect what we are going through. We read about the successful hero entrepreneur who made it and has lived to tell the tale about how grand it was. We find how-to books that explain what we should be doing (as though we had never thought of those ideas ourselves). It is rare to find truthful stories about how hard things can be, even in the best companies. This can make us feel alone—we feel like we are the only ones having these problems, and we are the only ones who can't figure out how to make them work.

Even though your story, your issues, your company, your product, or your service might not be exactly like the ones in this book, we hope these pages provide a reflecting pond where you can witness yourself and your company. Join us in trying to see clearly, hold lightly, laugh loudly, take the next step, and offer or welcome that helping hand. And then tell your story— all of it. It's important!

Index

About Social Venture Network

SVN transforms the way the world does business by connecting, leveraging, and promoting a global community of leaders for a more just and sustainable economy.

Since its founding in 1987, SVN has grown from a handful of visionary individuals into a vibrant community of five hundred business owners, investors, and nonprofit leaders who are advancing the movement for social responsibility in business. SVN members believe in a new bottom line for business, one that values healthy communities and the human spirit as well as high returns.

As a network, SVN facilitates partnerships, strategic alliances, and other ventures that promote social and economic justice. SVN collects and promotes best practices for socially responsible enterprises and produces unique conferences that support the professional and personal development of business leaders and social entrepreneurs.

Please visit www.svn.org for more information on SVN membership, initiatives, and events.

About the Authors

Margot Fraser is the founder and former CEO, president, and majority shareholder of Birkenstock USA. She retired from active leadership in 2002. The company is the sole importer of Birkenstock footwear in the United States and sells to more than 3,005 retailers, including 200 licensed, privately owned stores. When she started the busi-ness out of her home in 1967, ergonomic, functional footwear was unknown in the United States and was met with resistance and ridicule. Her belief in the product, and her undying conviction that others would recognize its value once they could get them on their feet, helped her persevere and slowly educate the public about the importance of foot health. This helped to establish a new category of footwear—Casual Comfort— an accomplishment that led to her induction into the National Shoe Retailers Hall of Fame. In the same year she was named the Ernst & Young Northern California Entrepreneur of the Year. She accomplished all that without any prior formal business education. She had only to follow her vision and common sense. However, continued learning was important to her. She finally attended the Executive Program for Smaller Companies at the Graduate School of Business, Stanford University, and returned for an intensive marketing course the following year. She established an ESOP at her company as a way to share the profits with her employees. She also used it as an exit strategy.

PHOTO: ILKA HARTMANN

Five years later, the ESOP acquired all the remaining shares and sold the business to the German manufacturer two years after that, dissolving the ESOP. Margot currently serves on the boards of the Presidio College of Management in San Francisco and the Family Service Agency of Marin in San Rafael. She speaks at conferences, women's groups, and business incubators to encourage new entrepreneurs to take the leap into an independent future.

Lisa Lorimer is the former CEO, president, and majority owner of Vermont Bread Company in Brattleboro, Vermont. She sold a majority stake in her company to the private equity firm Charterhouse Group and partnered with it to create the largest natural and certified organic baked-goods company in the United States. The  company has been renamed Charter Baking Company and services supermarkets and natural product stores under the brands of Vermont Bread, Baldwin Hill, The Baker, Rudi's Organic, and Matthew's All Natural, as well as private labels for various grocery store chains and other well-known national bakeries. During her twenty-three-year tenure at the company, Vermont Bread Company was the largest majority woman-owned business in the state and was listed as one of the top ten fastest growing companies in Vermont. Lisa is a graduate of the Owner/President Management Program at Harvard Business School and has served on the boards of Charter Baking Company, Vermont Businesses for Social Responsibility, Union

Institute & University/Vermont College, Vermont Community Foundation, the Women's Crisis Center, and Chittenden Bank. She speaks at conferences, seminars, leadership institutes, colleges, and business schools about lessons learned from growing her company.

About the Contributors

Carol Berry is the cofounder and former president/CEO of Putney Pasta, an all-natural gourmet pasta company. She started her business in 1983 with her then-husband, Jonathan Altman, in a renovated horse barn on their property in Putney, Vermont. Carol was responsible for the development of their innovative and unique line of upscale, vegetarian-filled pastas at a time when the market sold only meat-and-cheese-filled ravioli and tortellini. Their fillings and their quality separated their product from all other filled pastas in the marketplace. While raising a two-year-old child and running a business, Carol also served on the boards of the Vermont Manufacturing Extension Center, Connecticut River Valley Revolving Loan, Town of Chester Economic Development, and, for the last fifteen years, the Putney Food Coop, where she continues to serve. Carol sold her company in 2006 but has remained with the new group as the COO.

Gary Hirshberg, the husband of Meg Hirshberg and the father of three teenage yogurt eaters, is chairman, president, and CE-Yo of Stonyfield Farm, the world's leading organic yogurt producer, based in Londonderry, New Hampshire. Gary joined Stonyfield Farm a few months after its start in 1983. Initially he also directed the Rural Education Center, the small organic farming school from which Stonyfield was spawned. Previously, in addition to serving as a trustee of the farming school Gary had served as executive director of the New Alchemy Institute—a research and education center dedicated to organic farming, aquaculture, and renewable energy.

A New Hampshire native, Gary was one of the first graduates of Hampshire College in Amherst, Massachusetts, has received eight honorary doctorates, and has won numerous awards for corporate and environmental leadership. He serves on several corporate and nonprofit boards including Honest Tea, Applegate Farms, the Full Yield, Peak Organic Brewing Company, Stonyfield Europe, Dannon Company, Danone Communities Fund, and Climate Counts. He is also chairman and cofounder of O'Naturals, a chain of natural fast-food restaurants. In his spare time, he also serves as president of the Express Soccer Club and coaches a girls' under-seventeen premier travel soccer team, which keeps him humble and certain that he still has much to learn. For the past twenty-six years, Gary has overseen Stonyfield Farm's phenomenal growth, from its infancy as a seven-cow organic farming school to its current $240 million in annual sales. Stonyfield has enjoyed a compounded annual growth rate of 26.1 percent for more than eighteen years by consistently producing a great-tasting product and using innovative marketing techniques that blend the company's social, environmental, and financial missions. In 2001, Stonyfield Farm entered into a partnership with Groupe Danone, and in 2005, Gary was named managing director of Stonyfield Europe, a joint venture between the two firms with brands in Ireland and France and more in development.

Joe O'Connell is the founding owner of Creative Machines, a nine-person company that makes interactive museum exhibits, public art, and simple machines to help the neediest people around the world. Although (over) educated in the liberal arts, Joe is basically a maker at heart—someone who compulsively has to put things together and gradually expands the materials and processes he works with. He grew up in New Jersey, making all sorts of gadgets in his parents' basement. When he and his sisters were young, their parents built them each a workbench, gave them tools and piles of materials, and encouraged them to make things. Joe began Creative Machines in 1997 to make museum exhibits. A few years later he began using the resources of his company to make public art in order to explore new ideas and reach more diverse audiences. Joe's artwork often involves technology and is beautiful at first glance but yields deeper rewards with sustained engagement. Many of his sculptures (and indeed his entire business) are powered by photovoltaic arrays. In a step partly triggered by recent travels, Joe has turned toward making machines and art for the world's most needy. He is moving toward new forms of art and machines that can emerge only in places out of the mainstream.

Tom Raffio is president and CEO of Northeast Delta Dental, a provider of dental benefits to individuals and organizations in New Hampshire, Vermont, and Maine. The forty-eight-year-old, 180-person firm, which has offices in all three of the states in which it provides dental insurance coverage, has many measures in place to help its employees do just that. His company continues to have a 60 percent market share in New Hampshire, Maine, and Vermont, a market of over three million people. When Tom took over, the company had only a 15 percent market share. In this highly competitive business, providers get contracts for just one year. Nine months later they need to resell the organizations on why they should continue to use Northeast Delta Dental instead of Blue Cross or any of the other large competitors. The industry average for renewals is 80 percent; Northeast Delta Dental's rate is 97 percent. Tom feels most firms treat the customer like a commodity and when this happens, customers focus only on price. Tom uses customer service as a long-term strategy that continues to work.

Marie C. Wilson is founder and president of the White House Project, cocreator of Take Our Daughters and Sons to Work Day, and author of *Closing the Leadership Gap: Add Women, Change Everything* (Penguin, 2008). She left the Ms. Foundation in 2004 after two decades to devote her full energy to the White House Project. Over the past ten years, under Marie's direction, the White House Project has led groundbreaking research and program initiatives that work to fill the leadership pipeline with women. In 2004, the organization launched the Vote, Run, Lead training program, which engages women in the political process as voters, as activists, and as candidates for political office. Marie has also led the organization's efforts to expand women's leadership outside the political arena. In 2005, the White House Project launched SheSource.org, an online database that connects high-level female experts to top news media outlets. It also founded the Corporate Council, a group of senior executive women who are active agents of change within their corporations. To bring women's leadership and perspectives into the debate around national security, Marie spearheaded the organization's Real Security Initiative, which was a driving force behind the International Women Leaders Global Security Summit. To honor the culture changers who have brought positive images of women's leadership to the American public through film, television, theater, sports, and advertising, the White House Project hosts its annual EPIC (Enhancing Perceptions in Culture) Awards each spring in New York City. A leading advocate and voice on women's issues, Marie is the recipient of numerous awards and honors. She is a board member of the Women Donors Network and also a member of the Women's Leadership Board at Harvard's John F. Kennedy School of Government. She is a regularly featured blogger on the *Huffington Post* and appears frequently as an expert commentator and guest on programs and networks including *Good Morning America*, *Today*, National Public Radio, BBC, MSNBC, Lifetime, CNN, Fox, and ABC. Born and raised in Georgia, Marie served on the Des Moines city council. She has five children and four grandchildren and resides in New York City.

Values-Driven Business
How to Change the World, Make Money, and Have Fun
Ben Cohen and Mal Warwick

Ben & Jerry's cofounder Ben Cohen and Social Venture Network chair Mal Warwick team up to provide you with a complete guide to running your business for profit *and* personal satisfaction. This practical, down-to-earth book details every step in the process of creating and managing a business that will reflect your personal values, not force you to hide them. It includes a self-assessment tool to determine what it will take to start a values-based business or transform your company into one, as well as scores of real-world examples and practical suggestions.

$16.95, paperback, 192 pages, ISBN 978-1-57675-358-3
$11.87, PDF ebook, ISBN 978-1-57675-951-6

True to Yourself
Leading a Values-Based Business
Mark Albion

How do you build a company that serves people and the planet and turns a profit? What do you do when you believe that business should serve the common good, but everyday business pressures—meeting payroll, battling competition, keeping customers and investors happy—are at a fever pitch? The author of the *New York Times* bestseller *Making a Life, Making a Living* provides tools as well as advice from seventy-five forward-looking leaders to help you combine profit with purpose, margin with mission, value with values.

$16.95, paperback, 192 pages, ISBN 978-1-57675-378-1
$11.87, PDF ebook, ISBN 978-1-57675-950-9

Marketing That Matters
10 Practices to Profit Your Business and Change the World
Chip Conley and Eric Friedenwald-Fishman

Award-winning marketers Chip Conley and Eric Friedenwald-Fishman prove that "marketing" is not a dirty word—instead, it's key to advancing both the value and values of any business. They offer ten innovative marketing techniques—from discovering how customers make decisions to building committed communities of customers, employees, and strategic partners who will spread the word about your company—that will help you engage your customers and potentially change the world.

$16.95, paperback, 216 pages, ISBN 978-1-57675-383-5
$11.87, PDF ebook, ISBN 978-1-57675-964-6

Growing Local Value

How to Build Business Partnerships That Strengthen Your Community
Laury Hammel and Gun Denhart

Turn your business into a good citizen and you can help ensure its success *and* contribute to making your community a great place to live and work. Hanna Andersson founder Gun Denhart and BALLE cofounder Laury Hammel show how you can leverage every aspect of your business—product creation to employee recruitment, vendor selection, capital raising, and more—to benefit both the community and the bottom line.

$16.95, paperback, 192 pages, ISBN 978-1-57675-371-2
$11.87, PDF ebook, ISBN 978-1-57675-960-8

Values Sell

Transforming Purpose into Profit Through Creative Sales and Distribution Strategies
Nadine A. Thompson and Angela E. Soper

In this practical and inspiring guide, Nadine Thompson and Angela Soper draw on real-world examples to detail concrete steps for designing sales and distribution strategies that fit the needs, habits, and interests of your target customers. They show how to turn your stakeholders into enthusiastic partners by ensuring that all your relationships—with your salespeople, other employees, your customers, and your suppliers—are beneficial and fulfilling on more than just an economic level.

$16.95, paperback, 192 pages, ISBN 978-1-57675-421-4
$11.87, PDF ebook, ISBN 978-1-57675-520-4

Mission, Inc.

The Practitioner's Guide to Social Enterprise
Kevin Lynch and Julius Walls, Jr.

A new breed of business is springing up across the land: social enterprises, whose primary purpose is to support the common good. Organized as for-profits, nonprofits, and everything in between, they see businesses as the means to a better world for all. Lynch and Walls, Jr., explore ten key paradoxes of social enterprises and, using their own hard-won experiences and those of twenty other social enterprise leaders, show how to navigate the extreme challenges and seize the tremendous opportunities these organizations present.

$16.95, paperback, 216 pages, ISBN 978-1-57675-479-5
$11.87, PDF ebook, ISBN 978-1-57675-618-8

ABOUT BERRETT-KOEHLER PUBLISHERS

Berrett-Koehler is an independent publisher dedicated to an ambitious mission: **Creating a World That Works for All.**

We believe that to truly create a better world, action is needed at all levels—individual, organizational, and societal. At the individual level, our publications help people align their lives with their values and with their aspirations for a better world. At the organizational level, our publications promote progressive leadership and management practices, socially responsible approaches to business, and humane and effective organizations. At the societal level, our publications advance social and economic justice, shared prosperity, sustainability, and new solutions to national and global issues.

A major theme of our publications is "Opening Up New Space." They challenge conventional thinking, introduce new ideas, and foster positive change. Their common quest is changing the underlying beliefs, mindsets, institutions, and structures that keep generating the same cycles of problems, no matter who our leaders are or what improvement programs we adopt.

We strive to practice what we preach—to operate our publishing company in line with the ideas in our books. At the core of our approach is stewardship, which we define as a deep sense of responsibility to administer the company for the benefit of all of our "stakeholder" groups: authors, customers, employees, investors, service providers, and the communities and environment around us.

We are grateful to the thousands of readers, authors, and other friends of the company who consider themselves to be part of the "BK Community." We hope that you, too, will join us in our mission.

BE CONNECTED

Visit Our Website

Go to www.bkconnection.com to read exclusive previews and excerpts of new books, find detailed information on all Berrett-Koehler titles and authors, browse subject-area libraries of books, and get special discounts.

Subscribe to Our Free E-Newsletter

Be the first to hear about new publications, special discount offers, exclusive articles, news about bestsellers, and more! Get on the list for our free e-newsletter by going to www.bkconnection.com.

Get Quantity Discounts

Berrett-Koehler books are available at quantity discounts for orders of ten or more copies. Please call us toll-free at (800) 929-2929 or email us at bkp.orders@aidcvt.com.

Host a Reading Group

For tips on how to form and carry on a book reading group in your workplace or community, see our website at www.bkconnection.com.

Join the BK Community

Thousands of readers of our books have become part of the "BK Community" by participating in events featuring our authors, reviewing draft manuscripts of forthcoming books, spreading the word about their favorite books, and supporting our publishing program in other ways. If you would like to join the BK Community, please contact us at bkcommunity@bkpub.com.

BIBLIO RPL Ltée

G - MARS 2010